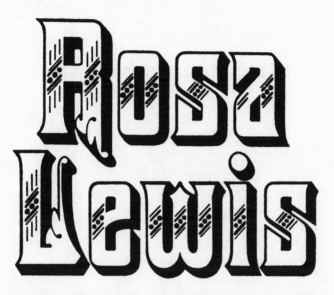

Rosa Lewis

An Exceptional Edwardian

Anthony Masters

ST. MARTIN'S PRESS
NEW YORK

TO JOHNNY WITH LOVE

Contents

Illustrations

Acknowledgements

I should like to thank the following who have been so helpful in bringing Rosa Lewis's complex personality to life: George Barrett, Chiquita Birkbeck, Dick Brennan, Dorothy Devon, Luis Dominguez, Daphne Fielding, Mrs I. G. Gibson, Major E. C. Hargreaves, Michael Harrison, John Hawkesworth, Michael Holroyd, Anna Howard, Mrs R. Izzard, Commander D. E. Jenkins, Robin McDouall, Jan Meekins, Nicholas Monsarrat, Betty Morrell, Malcolm Muggeridge, Conal O'Sullivan, Ethel Paull, Maud Puckering, Peter Quennell, McDonough Russell, Henry Rye, Sonia Stoakes, Tristan de Vere Cole, Michael Voysey, Brigadier J. H. P. Woodruffe, the *New Yorker* magazine, *Daily Express*, *Daily Mail*, *Daily Sketch*. Thanks also to Brenda Wood's efficient typing and Barbara Gough's intelligent editing.

Introduction

It had been a long decline. To many she appeared to be perpetually old, an Edwardian relic, an idiosyncratic old lady who was both loved and feared. Sitting in the high-backed chair in the Cavendish hallway or ensconced in her parlour, surrounded by admirers, Rosa Lewis lived strictly in the past. Her Edwardian heyday had ended with the death of one man and later with the deaths of thousands. The man was her beloved Edward VII, good old 'Kingy' whose various self-indulgences she had catered for so well. The thousands were her equally beloved 'boys' – the doomed young officers of the First World War.

Rosa said she had nothing to live for after 1918, and although the Bright Young Things and the young officers of the Second World War were compensations, they never filled the gap left by the crumbling away of the Edwardian era. Her answer to her growing feeling of isolation was to recreate that era in the Cavendish Hotel, and she even went to the extent of buying bits of one of the archetypes of Edwardiana – Dorchester House – to substantiate it. Rosa never failed to continue to dress in the style of that period – nor did she forget to apply the canons of its snobbish dissoluteness to the social life of her hotel.

The decline of Rosa Lewis was a grandiose and majestic affair. It lasted from 1918 until her death in 1952: thirty-four years of keeping the most remarkable hotel in Europe. Her rich clients regarded the Cavendish as a naughty nursery where they sowed their spurious wild oats and tippled their champagne, managed all the while by Rosa, their amoral nanny. In the last phase of the decline, from 1945 onwards, nanny failed to recognize many of her charges, often confusing them with Edwardian figures of the past. In the main they quickly accepted their new identities and

answered obediently to the name of some dead man. It was unwise
to get on the wrong side of her, for this would mean at best a
tongue-lashing, and at worst a command to leave the nursery for
ever.

Rosa's memory bank was her greatest strength and by the early
fifties she had almost totally withdrawn into it. Around her, the
old hotel deteriorated. Weeds and soot covered the flagstones of
the courtyard, and the fabric and fittings of the interior grew
shabbier by the hour. But Rosa never saw any of this. Sipping her
inevitable glass of champagne in her photograph-strewn parlour,
she saw a different world: the world of Edward VII, with its
dinner parties, its house parties, its groaning feasts, its 'liaisons'
and its frantic, exhausting, selfish good-timing. Rosa and her
catering service, her fleets of cooks and her culinary skill managed
the Edwardians' social pleasures to such an extent that she became
indispensable. Anybody who was anybody considered it unthinkable not to have Mrs Lewis organizing their social functions – and
these ranged from the highest families in the land to the Foreign
Office, and from statesmen to the King.

In her memory-strewn dotage Rosa saw other images – the
apartments she had kept for Edward's liaisons when he was Prince
of Wales; her close friendships with Lord Ribblesdale and Sir
William Eden; her 'seconding' to the Kaiser; her controversial
house at sacred Cowes; the buying of the Cavendish – all the
razamataz of being a figure of the utmost social importance. But
there were bitter memories, too – her disastrous arranged marriage,
and the way she had been used by the Edwardian court. Bitterest
of all, perhaps, was the fact that she had served and played hostess
to the cream of society and now in her old age she was childless
and alone – save for her devoted companion, Edith.

As Rosa's biography unravels, it will become obvious how she
in fact invented her own highly individual personality, and how
this synthetic identity eventually took her over. But for now it is
important to get one last glimpse of her as an old lady before she
is regenerated in the next section as a young girl. In a long
Edwardian dress she sits temporarily alone. It is mid-afternoon
and the Cavendish is between drinkers. Dust swirls in the filtered
light and the cluttered rooms with their country-house atmosphere
are silent. Time seems suspended and it is easy enough to share

Rosa's thoughts. Distantly the rooms are filled with hectic Edwardian gaiety. Women exchange effete small talk, encased in armour-like stays. Men talk about politics, about field sports, about gaming. Surreptitiously both groups eye each other – planning liaisons, planning the clandestine sexual excitement that made the enforced social graces of the age bearable. The tables are heavy with rich foods, expensive wine, and the champagne, of course, is flowing. But most important of all, nanny is there too. She can supply them with everything they need – food, wine, and arrangements.

Gradually the images dissolve, the echoes fade, and the Edwardian ghosts disappear. The once sumptuously furnished rooms return to their gentle decay and Rosa Lewis to her world of vibrant memory. She sleeps – and dreams – and is recalled many times to a past that, to her, is also the present.

ONE

A Start in Service
1867–87

'I learnt to think that it was not a stupid thing to cook.'
ROSA LEWIS

IN 1867, ROSA OVENDEN WAS BORN INTO A MID-VICTORIAN world of gathering material prosperity. Industrial production and foreign trade were well ahead of those of other countries, agricultural land was producing over seventy-five per cent of Britain's corn requirements, railway building was inexorably moving forward, and new industries, such as shipbuilding, were booming. As a result the upper and middle classes were happily complacent, whilst the lower classes remained uncomplainingly, acceptingly poor. But this complacency was not to go unchallenged and indeed its very presence induced bitter attack from such writers as Matthew Arnold, Thomas Carlyle and Charles Dickens. If these could be termed the radicals of the age, then the typical reactionaries and setters of moral and material style were represented by the self-satisfaction of Palmerston, Macaulay and the irrepressible Samuel Smiles. A few years before Rosa's birth, Samuel Smiles's *Self Help* appeared (20,000 copies sold in the first year of publication, 1859, and 130,000 over the next thirty years) which stimulated the publication of similar works on such auspicious subjects as 'Character', 'Thrift' and 'Duty'. It would be wrong, however, to describe the mid-Victorian age as totally unbenevolent or overtly materialistic. The combined forces of religion (an important factor in the lives of Victorian households) and humanism, deriving from liberalism and evangelism, gave the period a strong flavour of faith and conviction. But these qualities were largely to stay within the bastions of the upper and middle classes and did not reach out to affect or improve the lives of the poor.

London society, between the 1850s and the 1870s, was small enough to be commanded by a number of individuals whose activities and reputations were held in high respect. Ascot, Henley, the Derby, field sports, country house parties, the 'season', and the whole bandwagon of parade, show and etiquette, were worked at by their devotees as hard as any career. To be a Victorian hostess was a massively pressurized full-time job and with it went the administration of a battalion of servants. As if this wasn't enough, she also had to contend with 'being seen' – a very time-consuming and expensive business. A typical well-heeled lady of the times, Emily Charlotte Langtry, wrote in her biography, *The Days I Knew:* 'In the Victorian reign, the superbly-gowned women, wearing magnificent tiaras and shining with jewels, sitting waiting their turn in St James's Park in state coaches that were brought out only on these full-dress occasions, were a joy to behold. The bewigged coachmen, sitting in solitary glory on the resplendent hammercloths, and the powdered footmen in liveries heavy with silver or gold, standing on ledges at the back of these historic carriages, clinging to the embroidered straps, were also part of the show.'

Eighteenth-century society had not been large and there were only three or four hundred really important aristocratic families. These were, of course, mainly landowners. In London, Devonshire House and Bedford House were among the main centres of political activity and, in *Georgian England*, John Summerson described their 'immense public rooms and small squalid back bedrooms. They were not built for domestic but for public life – a life of continued entertaining in drawing-rooms, ante-rooms and 'eating rooms' where conversation would not be wholly ephemeral, where a sentence might be delivered which would echo round political England, where an introduction might mean the beginning of a career, or a deft criticism the dethronement of a policy.'

By the early nineteenth century the number of aristocratic families had increased and town houses and country seats proliferated. By the 1830s and 1840s privacy became an important factor in the social lives of upper- and middle-class families and public meeting-places and public show became unrespectable. There also seemed to be some fear of 'contamination' by rubbing shoulders with lesser breeds, and one country gentleman's wife had her own coach put on the train because 'it was important for her not to travel in a railroad carriage, as she might find herself sitting opposite someone with whom she was not acquainted'.

The vast masked balls of earlier times were becoming unpopular, club life was booming, drawing-room society was intense, and the debutante system was thriving amidst tortuous protocol.

In the main, the town houses were closed political camps, as demonstrated by the way Lady Palmerston ran Cambridge House. But in the years between 1850 and 1870 Lady Waldegrave's grandiose receptions at Strawberry Hill were open to Tories, Whigs and Radicals as well as to the leading literary and journalistic figures of the day. The all-powerful Lady Waldegrave also had a couple of country-houses in which to do similar entertaining, although her London season, during June and July of each year, was the most influential.

The atmosphere of the great country-house parties is best described by Lady Tweedsmuir in her book *The Lilac and the Rose:*

'In a gathering of people selected by a really clever hostess, there might be one or two Cabinet Ministers who welcomed the opportunity of quiet conversation, or there might be a Viceroy or high official from a far-off corner of the Empire, anxious to make someone in the government of the day realize a little more the difficulties of a particular experiment that Britain had delegated to him to carry out. These parties often included a diplomat home on leave, a painter, and almost certainly a musician who played to some of the company in the evenings. Beside these eminent people there was usually a sprinkling of women famous for their beauty or wit or both, who either gave the conversation a sparkling turn, or were wise enough not to interrupt good talk, and who accordingly sat looking statuesque or flowerlike.'

Rosa became involved in a rather more modern version of this society but nevertheless Lady Tweedsmuir successfully conveys the kind of atmosphere and social structure that Rosa saw – and quickly learnt both to dominate and, at times, to manipulate.

The village of Leyton, now a grey London suburb, was a far cry from all the pomp and circumstance of London society. Rosa's parents, William and Eliza Ovenden, were lower middle class, and William was originally a watchmaker and repairer. This was not a trade which flourished in Leyton, despite the fact that large country houses littered the Essex marshes. But their occupants would have selected their time-pieces in London, not Leyton, and the rest of the village's inhabitants would not be in a financial position to buy anything but the cheapest watches. Realizing that he could make only the most meagre living as a watchmaker, or chronometer-maker, as he preferred to be called, William Ovenden opened a Leyton branch of his brother's London-based undertaking business.

The trades of watchmaking, jewellery, and undertaking tended to go together in mid-Victorian times and indeed the Victorian age itself was the real heyday of the undertaker. Increasing wealth dictated lavish funerals. Fashion also dictated that each mourner, for instance, should be provided with a gold mourning-ring, engraved with the name of the deceased and some suitable 'in memoriam' legend. Hatchments were also required to elaborate the occasion. These were lozenge-shaped shields, depicting coats of arms, which were not only hung on the walls of the house above and below the death chamber but also covered the sides of the hearse as the body was conveyed to its final resting place. Black-edged mourning cards, funeral stationery, fancy coffins, silver plate – a vast paraphernalia of direct or sub-contracted work made the undertaking industry a highly profitable business.

William Ovenden, however, was not a mercenary man. His squandering was extravagant, although he had no particular vices on which to spend his money. His nine children all lived, which was unusual for the Victorian age, and this fact did not help the family finances either. When Rosa was two, William sold the three cottages he had gradually acquired and bought a one-storey shop and attendant living accommodation. This move made for highly cramped conditions and it is clear that Rosa did not enjoy the hurly-burly of family life, nor did she retain any particular affection or respect for either her parents or her brothers and sisters. She bore her childhood unresentfully but, with her restless personality, instinctively longed to get away from the ordered, routine boredom of her apathetically viewed existence.

There was Spanish and perhaps Jewish blood in the family, but essentially Eliza and William Ovenden were of traditional yeoman stock and had no ideas above their accepted station in life. Their Protestant religious views were orthodox and having been introduced through these benevolent but inactive channels, Rosa always retained a liking for the superficialities of church-going. Her parents' faith was merely conventional – part of the rhythm of their daily lives. William Ovenden's main economy in this area was to christen a batch of his children as a job lot, and records show that on 27 June 1869 at the Leyton parish church of St Mary the Virgin, Rosa and Lucy, daughters, and Frederick, son, of William Edwin and Eliza Ovenden, were all baptized together.

Rosa was the Ovendens' fifth child and went to Board School when she was about eight or nine years old. If she didn't feel much warmth for her family, she felt considerable warmth for the Board School headmistress, a Miss Lee. It is clear that Miss Lee responded to the child's native intelligence and wit, and unlike her parents, was able to channel some of it constructively. Miss Lee also appears to have had a good deal of charisma, and it was a fact of Rosa's personality, even at this age, that she tended to admire and to imitate the charismatic – and the more dominant, cantankerous or eccentric they were, the better. The Board School system was then in its infancy, and the local National school – a free primary school – was over-full. Miss Lee's establishment was in Leytonstone, which at that time was a separate village about two miles distant from Leyton but is nowadays joined to it as one entity.

At twelve Rosa left school because her father realized that she had now come to an age when she could make her own contribution to the rocky family finances. In an interview with an American journalist, Mary Lawton, who later wrote it up in her book *Queen of Cooks – And Some Kings*, (published in New York in 1926) Rosa shows clear if clinical insight into her apathy towards her family:

'My mother was a very simple woman, my brothers had to help support the house. One brother I liked very much, but the eldest one I didn't like at all. You see I was not a favourite child. I was not an affectionate person, and I was very independent. I did not want to be a cook then. I wanted to be a governess – I wanted to teach people how to live and what to do. This is what I had in mind, and I thought it was all so dreadful for my mother to be dependent on my brothers, and for the men to

take all the time about what they did to support the family –
it being their duty as well as their privilege.

Three meals a day in a middle class family is a terrible thing –
all the complaints of the family, every meal – and the only
surprise or excitement when you break in a window, burn up a
house or commit a murder. You see my brothers grumbled
about helping to support the family. I used to say: 'Of course,
men *always* talk about what they do! They must make a fuss
about it to be appreciated!' Then I would have a thrashing for
that. You see, they used to thrash me for saying these things –
which was only telling the truth, after all. But I never would
cry or show what I felt, and I never would kiss any of them –
never. I used to hold my breath till my nose bled and frighten
them all to death. I found out it would frighten them, so I did
it, because I never would cry, and would not mind what they
did to me; but I never could understand any of them.'

Michael Harrison, an earlier biographer (in *Rosa*, published by
Peter Davies in 1962) makes the comment that Miss Lee lived to
see 'her most famous pupil achieve a social eminence surely
beyond the dreams of even the most dedicated Board School
headmistress or even the most ambitious Board School scholar'.
Frankly, if Miss Lee had been any kind of decent and objective
school-teacher, she would have been horrified at the 'social
eminence' Rosa achieved in the rackety ambience of the Cavendish and its self-indulgent clientele. At twelve Rosa was an ambitious, independent and coldly self-contained young woman.
She felt she needed nobody, and she placed trust in her own great
energy and instinctive intelligence. The world she was about to
encounter was a rich, complacent, blinkered and benevolent one.
It was also ripe for plundering.

Rosa did not become a 'governess'. Instead, in 1879, she entered
domestic service in the house of a traditional middle-class
Victorian family. Mr and Mrs Ralph Musgrave of No. 3 Myrtle
Villas were classic *Diary of a Nobody* types. He worked in the city,
she ran the house and took an interest in good works such as the
overseas Missions. Rosa was employed as a general servant and
received a shilling a week. Her employer insisted on her wearing

her hair in a plait and also insisted she wore a long dress, presumably to discourage any possibility of admirers. The Musgraves were a singularly conventional couple and their standards were of staggering superficiality. They were not, however, atypical of their age. The specific routine of their domestic time-table mirrored the specific routine of their lives – lives that were very much governed by the style and etiquette of the time. Leyton was still a village but was also well on its way to becoming a suburb. In middle-class suburbs the rules of etiquette were strongly observed and it is more than likely that Mrs Musgrave's social life followed a similar kind of pattern to that described by W. MacQueen Pope in his book *Back Numbers: A Disturbance of the Dust of Yesteryear*. He pointed out that a wife from a smaller house in the area might be invited to a larger house, but:

> 'She would not be honoured by an invitation to the At Home Day which might be the Tuesday, first Wednesday, or third Thursday of the month. Not that invitations were issued for such functions. Friends knew that was the day on which the lady of the house was officially at home and it was therefore good form to call. She would inform new acquaintances whom she considered worthy, what her "Day" was. It was also engraved on her visiting cards . . . knowing the day and being sure you would be welcome or at least expected you called as if duty bound. The residents of the lesser roads knew all about these days, they had their own – but they never called then. They knew they were not of the inner circle. When they called it was on an "off" day and by appointment. They had tea downstairs from an earthenware teapot, not in the drawing-room from the silver teapot.'

Poor Mrs Musgrave probably spent hours worrying about breaches of etiquette and no doubt in her wildest nightmares she saw herself appearing unannounced, uninvited and unwanted at an inner-circle tea party.

Rosa's life at 3 Myrtle Villas was, to say the least, arduous. But despite its rigours, she lost herself in an interior life that was partly shelter from acute boredom, partly preparation for the future. 'I always had a great deal in my head, even then – much to the annoyance of everybody else – and always said the wrong thing at the wrong time,' she told Mary Lawton. 'But never mind what I felt – I wouldn't let them know it. I kept it to myself.'

Much of Rosa's renowned physical energy was stimulated by her chores at the Musgraves', which are worth cataloguing in all their arduousness. Her working day began at 6 am in the summer and at 5.30 am in the winter. Its schedule was as follows:

Before breakfast
Clean grates, sort the ashes, lay new fires, light them. Tidy rooms downstairs, wash linoleum and tiled hall, sweep stair-coverings and carpets. Cook breakfast, lay table, scrub and wash front door steps, polish front door knob, key-plate and letter slot. Await arrival of Musgraves for breakfast at 7.30 am.

Morning
Take instructions from Mrs Musgrave. Preparation of shopping list. Then wash breakfast dishes, empty chamber-pots, clean and polish furniture, clean the windows, sills, forks, spoons, prepare the lunch and lay the table.

Afternoon
Wash up lunch dishes. Short rest. Change from grey or pink morning uniform to black afternoon uniform. Prepare tea. Serve and clear away. Wash up. Prepare dinner for 7 pm sharp.

Evening
Clear table at 8 pm. Wash up. Tidy kitchen. Lay out night-cap (cocoa and biscuits). Bed at 9 pm.

Mrs Musgrave had little to do during the course of the day, except presumably worry about the problems of her social life. There is no indication that the couple had any children. Mr Musgrave was known by Rosa (and all tradesmen) as 'the Master', and they both looked upon their servant as a totally insensitive being. They presumably felt that she lacked physical feelings as well, for she was not allowed to use the bathroom in which the Musgraves wallowed in their once-weekly baths. She was considered 'too young' to need cleansing.

There were, of course, other duties which Rosa had to perform for the ritualistic Musgraves. There was the involved Victorian Monday wash, with the outhouse copper, soap and scrubbing board. There was Church on Sundays, to which Rosa was expected to accompany the Musgraves, leaving before the end of the service so that the ponderous Sunday lunch would be cooked and served on time. Therefore, to the Musgraves, Rosa was a sub-person, who needed scant spiritual, hygienic and physical comfort and certainly should at all costs be kept away from men and books. In the case of the former, Rosa had just escaped from a world of chauvinistic men, so this deprivation meant little. But books, which the Musgraves no doubt secretly believed might encourage the working classes to sedition, were adrenalin to her. Slowly at first, and then with greater ease, she read a vast diet of middle-brow – and lesser brow – literature.

Rosa did not resent the Musgraves for she had escaped from a family background she despised. In a sense she had independence – her own room and her own world, into which she could withdraw completely, only viewing the mechanical Musgraves as a remote 'them'.

Rosa stayed with the Musgraves for four years. She felt neither bitterness nor anger over the poor conditions under which she worked; it was a predicament of her times, something she could not have avoided. Many thousands of her contemporaries lived under exactly the same conditions – or in some cases considerably worse. But in 1883, when she was sixteen, Rosa gave in her notice to a surprised Mrs Musgrave, who presumably had assumed that she had a servant for life. Nevertheless, she gave Rosa a good reference, which was important, for Rosa's next position was as under-kitchenmaid (twelve shillings and sixpence per week) in the household of the exiled heir to the French throne, the Comte de Paris. It was a humble enough job – but in a very aristocratic household. She came by the job through the influence of an uncle, who was a friend of the Comtesse de Paris's chef at Sheen House in Mortlake. No longer did Rosa aspire to be a governess and to 'teach people how to live and what to do'. Over the past four years of her desperately ordered life with the Musgraves, she had taught *herself* how to live and what to do. For she had realized, in the little free time she had been given, that there was absolutely no way in which she could become a head-mistress. She was in domestic service and her ambitions could only be achieved through that. Her family were poor and narrow. They could pull no further strings nor bring any influence to bear.

She had the bare rudiments of education and no means of earning a living to pay for more. Nevertheless she was determined that she would not remain a lowly figure for long. She would work through the domestic-service structure until she became a cook. A cook who was independent – and powerful.

By the early 1880s English society was a strong three-class system, at the bottom of which was considerable, obvious poverty and at the top end of which was hard-working, never-ending gaiety. In the middle, social aspirations ran high and there was an unyielding allegiance to standards, to duty and the ideology of the devoted, close-knit Victorian family. Over two million of the working-class population were employed as domestic servants, and this system did not begin to disintegrate until the First World War; it did not wholly disappear until the end of the Second World War. In an audience with Queen Victoria in 1870, shortly before his death, Dickens stated that the division of classes in England would improve in time. Later, on Dickens's death, Victoria said, 'He felt sure that a better feeling, and much greater union of classes would take place in time. And I pray earnestly it may.' Perhaps this sounds out of character for this idiosyncratic and prejudiced woman, but in fact she was perfectly aware of the unequal distribution of wealth in the country and the considerable structural reorganization the country needed. But radicalism, with its revolutionary aspect, she feared, and gradual change she found more acceptable. As for the Prince of Wales, Sir Philip Magnus (in his biography, *King Edward the Seventh*) remarks that he was 'eager to see suffering relieved but he equated socialist remedies with revolution. He feared the risk of damage to the organic structure of a hierarchical society which he regarded as divinely ordained.'

Already the activities of the Prince of Wales had taken a markedly different turn from those of his mother and the strict behavioural code laid down for him in his infancy by Prince Albert. Over-disciplined, over-protected, lonely and never his parents' favourite, it was predictable enough that Edward, on reaching maturity, should let rip. He was aware of being unloved and further aware that his parents' intense love for each other had left little emotion to spill over on to their children. At fifteen, on a visit to Paris, he asked the Empress if he could stay: 'They don't want us, and there are six more of us at home.' Indeed, his own mother wrote harshly of him in the desperate emotion surrounding Albert's death in 1861. The young Edward had been involved in an affair with an actress and had admitted all to Albert at Cambridge, where that worthy and deadly dull disciplinarian caught a chill which ended in the fatal bout of typhoid fever. 'Oh that boy', Victoria wrote, somehow linking the conduct of her son with her husband's death. 'Much as I pity, I never can, or shall, look at him without a shudder.'

It was no small wonder that Edward, also excluded from all political involvement, did not turn his vast acreage of spare time to more demonic use. But it was his past training and his belief in the 'divinity' of his position that saved him from turning into the darkest of Regency rakes. Instead, he plunged into a round of pleasure, indulging in vast meals, considerable quantities of alcohol, and the social whirl of Ascot, Cowes, Balmoral and innumerable house parties that nearly bankrupted those who gave them.

It is of interest to pause at this stage and contrast a typical day during an Edwardian house-party with the already documented typical day in Rosa's life *chez* Musgrave:

10 am.
Rise to huge breakfast involving some thirty different dishes including porridge, cream, coffee, cold drinks, Indian and China tea, bacon, ham, sausages, poached and scrambled eggs, devilled kidneys, haddock, tongue, pressed beef and ham, cold roast pheasant, partridge, grouse, ptarmigan, fruit, scones, toast, marmalade, honey, jam.

11–1.30 pm.
Field sports (depending on location of house party).

1.30 pm.
Lunch, involving at least eight courses.

2.30–4 pm.
Field sports with women as spectators.

4–4.30 pm.
Change for tea.

4.30 pm.

Tea, involving sandwiches, bread and butter, toast, jam, cakes, and lobster salad if the Prince of Wales was in attendance.

5.30–7.30 pm.

Stultifying conversation, practical jokes and paper games.

7.30 pm.

Change for dinner.

8.30 pm.

Dinner, involving at least twelve rich courses with appropriate wines. A sample menu might include soup, fish, two consecutive entrées, joint, game, sweet, savouries, bread and cheese, mustard and cress – to say nothing of dessert, fruit, nuts and cheese. The latter was meant to clear the palate so as to allow serious after-dinner drinking.

10 pm.–2 am.

Bridge, baccarat (illegal but much played, particularly if the Prince of Wales was a guest).

2 am.

Sandwiches, devilled chicken, whisky and soda.

Nevertheless, it should be pointed out that despite the invidious comparison between all this feasting and Rosa's own work-schedule, the Edwardian hostess and her guests worked almost as hard as Rosa did – but to enjoy themselves. Enjoyment was a task, empty hours had to be filled, food and entertainment were vast undertakings. Boredom, always the enemy, was relieved by a large number of practical jokes, many of them very laboriously planned. The Prince of Wales was particularly partial to these, and continually devised them – another sign of his arrested childhood development.

In March 1863, with Queen Victoria in full mourning for Albert, Edward married Princess Alexandra, a daughter of the rather poor Danish royal family. He remained fond of her for the rest of his life and he also became a highly affectionate father to his children. Neither of these two factors, however, prevented him from womanizing to a heavy degree and over the years the royal favourites included 'La Goulue' (the dancer at the Moulin Rouge who was immortalized by Toulouse Lautrec – a favourite who particularly horrified Queen Victoria); the celebrated Catherine Walters of *Skittles*; Frances, Countess of Warwick; Lily Langtry; Sarah Bernhardt; the famous Mrs Keppel; and Mrs Agnes Keyser, amongst others.

In the same year, Edward was given a yearly allowance of £100,000, Marlborough House in London, and Sandringham in Norfolk. Marlborough House was to become very much part of Rosa's life and her culinary arts an essential factor in running such an establishment.

Scandal, however, was never very far away from the Prince of Wales, and gradually he began to lose popularity. Rumours of orgies in Paris, rumours of gambling debts, the Mordaunt divorce case (in which Lady Mordaunt claimed to have 'done wrong' with the Prince of Wales) and an outrageous request to use Lord Rosebery's London home as a place in which to 'entertain' the Prince's 'actress friends' merely heralded other scandals – the most serious of which was to be the Tranby Croft affair.

The Prince of Wales is an important figure in Rosa's life and it must be emphasized that, with his background, his actions were entirely predictable. He preserved an outward front of extreme dignity, did not encourage familiarity, and although he bankrupted many of his friends, he was capable of kind actions when pushed. His mother certainly grew fonder of him, but was terrified that he would wreck the dignified image of the monarchy that Albert had created. Indeed she was afraid that he would finally wreck the monarchy altogether. Complaining to her errant son in 1869, she told him, 'There is a *very* strong feeling against the luxuriousness and frivolity of society – and everyone comments on *my* simplicity.' She disapproved of his friends and their Jewish or commercial roots, later pointing out to him, 'If you ever become king, you will find all these friends *most* inconvenient.' Needless to say, Edward totally ignored all his mother's complaints and warnings.

Despite all this, Edward's sense of duty was as strong as his sense of pleasure. It is true to say that his activities encouraged considerable discussion about ending the monarchy but it is also true that he fulfilled his public duties with admirable dignity and efficiency. Moreover, Victoria's withdrawal from her people after Albert's death did as much damage to the image of the monarchy

as Edward's over-involvement. Although often disapproved of by
the Church and the middle classes, he remained popular with the
working class, even through his most disastrous periods. The
good sportsman with the pretty woman and the big cigar was
found to be an acceptably remote and romantic image, and
'Good old Teddy!' was the proletarian shout. Keith Middlemas
in his biography, *Edward VII*, sums the situation up most
accurately: 'Edward's activities did not mould a new high
society, but they simply bestowed the patronage of royalty on the
fringe of the aristocracy that had scarcely bowed to the middle-
class ethic of morality and which looked for tradition to the
eighteenth-century style of "fast" living.'

Rosa's entry into the household of the Comte de Paris was the
beginning of a fast rise to the echelons of that 'fringe of the
aristocracy' discussed above. On a young girl of sixteen whose
staple reading diet must have been romance, the effete and
superficial Comte and Comtesse must have made a story-book
impression. The contrast between Sheen House and No. 3
Myrtle Villas was immense, and although she was under-kitchenmaid, which largely meant scrubbing floors all day, she must have
been favourably impressed not only by the whole ambience of
wealthy exiled monarchy but also by the very large staff that
served them. In fact the staff were almost like a heavily graded
industrial force whose job it was to provide a large number of
different services for a small group of remarkably critical con-
sumers. It is not on record exactly how many servants the exiled
Comte employed and it is unlikely that he had as large a staff as the
Duke of Portland had at Welbeck Abbey. Nevertheless it is
worth recording the pecking order at Welbeck as a comparison:

Kitchens and Services
Steward
Wine butler
Under butler
Groom of the chambers
4 royal footmen
2 steward's room footmen
Master of the servants' hall
2 page-boys

Head chef
Second chef
Head baker
Second baker
Head kitchen-maid
2 under kitchen-maids
Vegetable maids
3 scullery maids
Head stillroom maid
Hall porter
2 helpers (hall boys)
Kitchen porter
6 odd men

House and Personal Service
Head housekeeper
Duke's valet
Duchess's personal maid
Lady Victoria's personal maid
Head nursery governess
Tutor
French governess
Schoolroom footman
Nursery footman
14 housemaids

Mechanical Help in the Household
6 engineers (house and electric plant)
4 firemen (electric plant and steam heating)
Telephone clerk and assistant
Telegrapher
3 night-watchmen

Stable
Head coachman
Second coachman
10 grooms
20 strappers and helpers

Garage
Head chauffeur

15 chauffeurs
15 footmen (2 men on the box at all times)
2 washers

Estate Management
Estate manager (Duke's confidential clerk)
Secretary to the Duke

Chapel
Resident chaplain
Organist

Titchfield Library
Librarian
Clerk
Housemaids (for dusting)

Racing Stables
Stud groom
15 assistants

Gardens
6 house gardeners (subterranean greenhouses and house
   decorations)
30–40 gardeners
40–50 roadmen

Home Farm
Head farmer
15–20 men in vegetable gardens and orchards

Gymnasium
Head instructor
Japanese trainer

Golf course
Head greensman
10 helpers

Laundry cottage
Head laundress
12 laundresses

Window cleaners
Head window cleaner
2 assistants

The Comte de Paris, born in 1838, had gone into exile in England with his father in 1848. He was brought up at Claremont near Esher and bought Sheen House near Mortlake when he was twenty-one. In 1870 his two uncles returned to France, where they were allowed to become members of the National Assembly. In 1883 the Comte became head of the house of Bourbon and was, on this basis, accepted by the Royalist party as France's rightful king. Already the corpses of King Louis Philippe and his family had been returned to France and this, coupled with the Comte's acceptance by the Royalists, served to infuriate the Republicans. All this was, of course, happening while Rosa was working at Sheen House but there is no indication that she was particularly affected by these dramatic events – although they must have formed the bulk of the below-stairs gossip. The final crisis occurred in 1886 – the year before Rosa gave in her notice to the Comte de Paris.

There had been one royal marriage in France in 1885, and in 1886 the Comte de Paris married his daughter Marie Amélie in France to Don Carlos, Duke of Braganza and heir to the Portuguese throne. A massive reception was untactfully thrown by the Comte and every vital Royalist name was on the guest list. As a direct result the Republicans introduced a bill to expel from France the heads of the former reigning families and this was passed by both the Chamber of Deputies and the Senate on 11 June 1886. Twelve days later the Bonapartes left France and the next day the Comte de Paris returned to exile in Sheen House after only a brief stay in his native country. On landing at Dover the affronted and frustrated Comte told the English press that he was certain that the return of the monarchy was the only sure way to govern France – and that as a result of his expulsion he was putting himself at the head of the Royalist movement.

Meanwhile, Rosa was being promoted in the kitchens of Sheen House. She began washing up and absorbing the alien atmosphere of the household. She was the only English member of the staff and it was because of this that she was able to assimilate culinary French. She told Mary Lawton, 'The Comtesse de Paris was the most interesting woman in the world. There never was a better brought-up family in the world than hers. Every child had its two nurses, and every child was made to learn something –

something useful – to make a boot, cook a cake and so on.' In fact, the upbringing of the children sounds disastrous. The Comtesse was a strange masculine woman, a good shot, an excellent rider, a voracious cigar-smoker, and a domestic tyrant. Indeed, she seemed to specialize in making life as dull and disciplined as possible, particularly when, as Rosa went on to tell Mary Lawton: 'Why, she even put on her chemise at the same hour every day of her life, and all her family were never a minute late for Mass. And they knew this time this year, exactly what they were going to do at the same time next year.'

With relief one turns to the Comte, who seems to have been a man of more elastic personality. This is certainly underlined by the fact that the Prince of Wales regularly came to dinner at Sheen House. There is no doubt, however, that he came for the Comte and gormandizing, rather than to flick a lascivious eye at the butch Comtesse. Rosa first met Edward at a dinner party during the course of which she was called from the kitchen to sing 'God Bless the Prince of Wales' in the absence of a pianist. Rosa obliged the drunken company, was confused by the Prince of Wales for the cook, and later given a sovereign from a purse he apparently kept specifically for these occasions. It was largely as a result of this encounter that Rosa became more and more determined to be a cook in what she saw as the very best possible circles. There are several versions of this anecdote, however, mainly told by Rosa herself, and although there is little doubt that she did have such an encounter, not all the details seem consistent. In fact, most of Rosa's reminiscences, mainly related during her heyday at the Cavendish, are a curious mixture of what she would have liked to have taken place, what made a good anecdote, and a few small grains of ill-remembered truth.

Rosa spent five years altogether with the Comte de Paris and never made any mention in her interviews with Mary Lawton of the Comte's political problems. Maybe they really did pass her by – or maybe she was just more interested in the extraordinary world that surrounded her. She still sent part of her money home although it is clear that she didn't actually *go* home very much. She didn't spend all her time at Sheen House either. She was lent, as a well recommended kitchen-maid, to the Comte's uncle, the Duc d'Aumale, the son of Louis Philippe, historian, art-connoisseur, distinguished soldier and wit. He had a large palace at Chantilly in whose grounds were racing stables, a racecourse and a large amount of expensive blood-stock. Lakes and waterfalls studded the parkland around the château, which itself was moated. Greek temples and marble statues had been placed in the woodlands, deer were hunted with the Duke's personal hounds – in fact the entire set-up was rather like a red rag to an angry Republican. With great forethought, however, the Duke escaped into exile in 1886, when he offered to leave Chantilly to the Institut de France – a ploy that ensured he could at least continue his own life-style uninterrupted.

Rosa, having returned to England from what she considered was a fairy-tale, was then lent out again to another French exile – the Comte's son, the Duke of Orléans, at Sandhurst. There, she became a temporary cook. Such an elevation at twenty years old shows that she must have more than proved herself at Sheen House and Chantilly. It also meant that the French staff had conceived a great respect for a British would-be cook and a woman at that – which in those times was even more amazing than Rosa's own prowess. But Rosa was not merely developing practical abilities, she was also developing perception and a sense of awareness of other people. And because of her independence and ambition she was already learning to play the roles and assume the identities that her employers wanted. This is well illustrated by some very honest comments Rosa made to Mary Lawton:

'I learnt to think there that it was not a stupid thing to cook. I saw that the aristocracy took an interest in it, and that you came under the notice of someone that really mattered. It struck me it was far more interesting than a factory life; that you were not just one of a number of sausages! I saw they took an interest in me, their chefs and other people. I picked up what I could there – I taught myself. I worked every spare moment – I helped everybody else, and by helping everybody else I helped myself, because I picked the brains of the other people, and what they had got I soon got, so between the two I made a wonderful success.

You see, if I met a woman, or I went to a house, I would note by the painting over the door what kind of a woman she was.

Then I would create my conversation according to red, pink, blue or green – just as she wanted. I would know whether that woman's *clothes* were the most important thing in her life, or whether her *house* was the most important thing, or whether what she was going to *eat* was the most important thing, or whether *love* was the important thing. And then I would treat her accordingly. I learnt the great secret of life – humanity – understanding other people. A person who is not interested in art and colour, you don't waste your time on giving them that. You use your time and your money on the one thing which is to please that person. If they will only give you five shillings, you put into the five shillings the one thing that appeals to them.'

A cook was held in some esteem by the majority of households. After all, she was a vital figure and few wished to go hungry by upsetting her. Indeed the *Servants' Practical Guide* of 1880 advises caution. 'Some ladies stand in very much awe of their cooks, knowing that those who consider themselves to be thoroughly experienced will not brook fault-finding, or interference with their manner of cooking, and give notice on the smallest pretext. Thus, when ladies have a really good cook, they deal with her delicately, and are inclined to let her have her own way with regard to serving the dinner.' The *Guide* goes on to give more advice on how to deal with this the most precious of all servants and concludes: 'It is an understood thing that the cook has certain perquisites connected with her place, amongst others the dripping from the roast joints.'

In Jubilee Year, 1887, Rosa gave in notice to the Comte de Paris's secretary, received a glowing recommendation and armed with this, went to an agency. There she discovered that Lady Randolph Churchill needed a cook, to replace her already overworked chef on his days off. Now Rosa was entering the world of the English aristocracy and already, at twenty years old, she felt able to handle the situation. She was not lacking in confidence, nor was she lacking in guile. Above all she was determined to come 'under the notice of someone that really mattered'.

TWO

Noblesse Oblige

1887–1902

'I cooked because I loved to cook – the money didn't matter.'
ROSA LEWIS

LADY RANDOLPH CHURCHILL, NÉE JENNIE JEROME, WAS ONE of the principal society hostesses of the nineteenth century and to document her well-known life here would be purposeless. Sufficient to say that Rosa was principally drawn to her because she was the daughter of a self-made man – Leonard Jerome, of farming origins in Syracuse, who made and lost a number of fortunes on the New York stock exchange. Rosa joined the Churchill household and soon worked full time there at a period when serious problems had arisen. Although Randolph Churchill was now back in favour with the Prince of Wales after the latter's intransigence over the Aylesford divorce case, and this meant that he and Jennie were also back in the cream of the social swing, other matters did not bode so well. After a belligerent and overbearing career as Chancellor of the Exchequer and Leader of the House, Randolph had threatened to resign – and been forced to make good his threat. He was an overworked, sick man, who also, unbeknown to his wife, was suffering from syphillis. Having possibly had an affair with the Prince of Wales, the outstandingly beautiful Jennie had taken a lover – a spectacularly colourful Hungarian Count, Charles Kinsky. This was to compensate for the fact that she and Randolph now slept apart, and there was public speculation, much refuted by Randolph, that the couple were to separate. Kinsky, who had won the Grand National in 1883 riding his own horse Zoedone, was romantic, suitably rich and charismatic. He was hero-worshipped by Jennie's two sons, Winston and Jack, who had been greatly neglected by the aggressively career-minded Randolph. Originally Jennie, who was both intelligent and perceptive if socially aspiring, had been delighted by her husband's spectacular career in the Conservative party. Without it she realized that his natural Churchillian aggression would only seek an outlet in inter-family quarrels or more public slanging-matches, such as the Aylesford quarrel with the Prince of Wales.

So it was a very unplacid household that Rosa entered. However, as with the Comte de Paris, she was either too young or too much overawed to appreciate the situation, although there is no doubt that the servants' quarters were aflame with gossip. Rosa superficially took Jennie's side, imagining that Randolph treated her badly. It is true that he did not treat her particularly well, nor did he treat his own children particularly well, but despite this, they had a deep fondness for each other and they worried continually about each other's health – and each other's peace of mind. Rosa told Mary Lawton: 'Lady Randolph Churchill only wanted a few things, but those things she wanted the most perfect, and perfect things to eat. She was one of the most perfect women herself that I have ever met. She always put all her money in a few things. I learnt that the first time I saw her. You knew very well that you could put all your money in one or two dishes for her, so long as they were perfectly cooked and the room was the right temperature, for instance.'

The Churchills' home, at 50 Grosvenor Square, was a mecca of social entertainment. Jennie liked a wide social mix and was ambitious in her invitations. She even extended a luncheon invitation to the vegetarian George Bernard Shaw, who replied tetchily: 'Certainly not. What have I done to provoke such an attack on my well-known habits?' With spirit, if not with subtlety, Jennie sent the great man this reply: 'Know nothing of your habits. Hope they are not as bad as your manners.' The entertaining was on the usual lavish scale and the Prince of Wales was an inveterate visitor, once things between him and Randolph had been patched up. Vast meals, taken with alcohol-clouded palates, were the order of the day, the fun was fast and frenetic, sexual needs were catered for and practical joking assumed near surreal qualities. Booby-traps, apple-pie beds, slapstick, horseplay, were never very far away, particularly when the Prince of Wales was around. His personal circle were particularly long-suffering, often wondering where and at whom the royal joker would strike next. Jennie, who could have been considered intellectually above such things, was far from adverse to them, and was known to have seated herself at a dinner party during the first year of Rosa's service, claiming that she was wearing a Jubilee bustle which played 'God Save the Queen' every time she sat down. Underneath her chair squatted a servant of the small variety with a musical box. The Prince of Wales was, no doubt, reduced to hysteria by this hilarious tribute to his mother, who would definitely *not* have been amused. Also present at the dinner party was the long-suffering Princess Alexandra who, though hardly a bad sport, was unlikely to have found Jennie's performance quite as hilarious as her husband did.

Rosa had now met the Prince of Wales on a number of occasions and he invariably praised the excellence of her cooking. She already knew his tastes from Sheen House, where the Churchills must also have dined from time to time. Rosa told Mary Lawton that the Prince of Wales 'liked very simple food. Whatever it was, it had to be very plainly cooked. If he had a pear, it would be a perfectly plain pear – no colouring; and the only flavouring he liked with his fruit was kirsch. He also liked very plain boiled bacon and flat [kidney] beans; and he was especially fond of plain boiled truffles. He didn't like anything coloured, or anything sloppy, or anything that would spill down his shirt-front; just simple plain cooking, and truffles I used to do specially for him. If a dinner party was being given in his honour, this dish used always to be there every time, just served in a white serviette.'

Despite her penchant for Jennie, Rosa was not to stay with her for very long – her ambition wouldn't allow it. Apart from being such a very successful cook, she was now fast becoming a successful kitchen administrator. Considering the paraphernalia of the meals of the era, good administration was vital, and many cooks had already broken down over the complexity and sheer size of the menus.

She left the Churchill establishment for Mrs Charles Lawrence and then for 'some other old girl in Chester Square'. This anonymous woman took the decision that Rosa was too young to be cooking her meals and called in Rosa's family to take her back to the doubtful sanctuary of Leyton. She evaded them successfully and then began to work in a variety of kitchens belonging either to the upper middle classes or the aristocracy. But the aristocracy was not always English, and it was in the kitchens of the American Low family from Savannah that Rosa learnt a good deal about

Southern-style cooking from their black chef. However, it was in the house of Lord Savile, originally Augustus Lumley, that Rosa received the Establishment seal of approval – and was taught the social games-playing of the age. It was as a result of Lumley's manipulating that Rosa's career really took off. It also marked the start of what must have been a growing cynicism. Many later associates of Rosa, mainly those who stayed at the Cavendish, uneasily admit that Rosa had a strong contempt as well as a strong affection for the moneyed classes, be they Edwardians, the bright young things of the twenties and thirties, or the third generation of well-heeled layabouts who hung round the Cavendish in its decline after the Second World War.

Augustus Lumley was a Victorian 'fixer'. Ex-Household Cavalry, the impoverished Lumley became the Master of Cere-monies to Victoria's household. His job was to sort out who was socially acceptable and who was not. He made it his business to make London society aware that he was its social director, he gave the necessary seal of approval to social acceptability, and he also made everyone realize that he knew each coil of the social world intimately. He claimed to be all-seeing and all-knowing. Lumley recognized Rosa's talents at an early stage. He saw in her a brilliant cook, a superb administrator, and the ability to be discreet. Gentlemen's calling on ladies who belonged to other gentlemen, wife-swopping in country house parties, the Prince of Wales's sexual appetite – all were situations which required Rosa's management.

Lumley's reputation as a social mafioso was widespread and he was much feared. He was not rich – indeed he was very poor – but his gorgon-like position gave him the kind of power that no amount of money could buy. It was Lumley who secured the Rothschilds' social recognition, Lumley who could double the status of a deb by dancing with her, Lumley who could make or break anyone's social viability. It was also Lumley who invented code-words to clarify to others whether someone was acceptable or not. He chose 'Rose' and 'Cabbage', the first being derived from Rosa's name, the second being a vegetable about which she had an obsession. (She told Mary Lawton: 'What I have always done (which no other cook ever does) is to cook the potatoes, and the beans, and the asparagus *myself*. I do not give these to the charwoman or the scullery maid – or a person without brains – because they are more expensive than the meat, and more essential than anything else in the dinner. I would take more trouble with the cabbage than most people would with a chicken.') So when asked by the British Ambassador in Paris, Lord Lyons, to gauge the social respectability of someone who had called at the Embassy, Lumley sent back the code word 'Cabbage'. This meant that the chap was 'wrong'. A wrong 'un! If he'd been a right 'un, the code-word would have been 'Rose'. Rosa moved between three Lumley establishments – 38 South Street, Park Lane; Rufford Abbey, Ollerton; and Rushworth Lodge, Halifax.

It would be wrong to say that Rosa was seen by Lumley as the future proprietress of a high-class brothel. Nevertheless her discretionary talents were regarded by Lumley as a vital asset to his social manipulating. A good cook and a blind eye – a combination that he couldn't afford to lose, particularly in relation to the Prince of Wales and the Marlborough House set.

Her short but effective Lumley training scheme came to an end with a final instruction. As far as possible she was to confine her operations to bachelor or male-run households, a piece of social male chauvinism that must have considerably increased her contempt, although she at no point admitted to this. It must also have considerably enraged the instinctive feminism that had made her self-orientated and rather sexually withdrawn. She may in later years have slept with the aristocracy but at this point, in her early twenties, she considered men to be out for what they could get and women to be the victims – hence her superficial appraisal of the relationship between Jennie and Randolph Churchill.

Bearing in mind the 'bachelor or male-run households' instruction, Rosa worked for a young member of the Marlborough House set, Captain Duff, in his bachelor apartments at 1 Lennox Gardens, Pont Street; next in the country house near Liverpool of Major William Hall Walker, MP for Widnes; and then she broke with her new 'tradition' to work for the Asquiths. At this time, in the early 1890s, the political situation was increasingly less stable. Indeed, from the very beginning of the 1870s there had been social tension and various national and international crises, such as the Paris Commune, the frustration of the French monarchist restoration, the Boer War, the Phoenix Park murders and the London Dock Strike, as well as economic problems. All this made for a good deal of national insecurity and the Prince of Wales's more scandalous activities did not help the stability of the monarchy itself – that vital crutch to all classes of British people in times of stress and unease.

Nevertheless Queen Victoria herself came through as a symbol of stability. She was an institution that was rock-solid. The historian David Thompson, in his *England in the Nineteenth Century*, wrote of her: 'Just as the succession of unattractive Hanoverians had brought monarchy into jeopardy, so the succession of attractive monarchs from Queen Victoria onwards created a new type of royal authority, resting not on constitutional prerogatives or political activity, but on the psychological needs of nationalism and imperialism and on the love of the masses of what Bagehot called "nice and pretty events".'

Margot Asquith's political strivings are well known – but it was the insecurity on which these were based that Rosa detected. Asquith had been a widower and Margot only met his children after they were married, on 10 May 1894. Temperamentally quite different from Herbert Asquith, Margot wrote of this problem in her autobiography, when talking of her step-children:

> 'Tennants [her own maiden name] believed in appealing to the hearts of men, firing their imagination and penetrating and vivifying their inmost lives. ... The Asquiths – without mental flurry and with perfect self-mastery – believed in the free application of intellect to every human emotion. .... shy, self engaged, critical and controversial, nothing surprised them and nothing upset them. We were as zealous and vital as they were detached and as cocky and passionate as they were modest and emotionless.'

Apart from Rosa's ready association with the driving, striving, insecurities of Margot Asquith, there was another link between them that was to be a vital force in Rosa's life. Margot was the sister-in-law of Lord Ribblesdale, associate of the Prince of Wales and Master of the Queen's Buckhounds. Later Lord Ribblesdale was to become of the greatest importance to Rosa.

In regard to Margot Asquith, Rosa told Mary Lawton: 'Of course, I've a word about Mrs Asquith and what I have to say

about her is that she's very much better than people give her
credit for. If she promised her leg ... she still pays for that leg,
because all her "in-laws" with their children are all poor, and
she must always be doing for them.'

This, no doubt, was an oblique reference to Margot's strongly
developed social conscience and concern for the moral and
material welfare of the poor.

Here then was another influence on Rosa – a powerful one.
And it was an influence that once again tended to make Rosa
admire the independence and fortitude of women. She could have
been talking of herself in later years when she said of Margot
Asquith, 'but she has an aggressive manner. Her great failure was
her over-anxiety to get enough money in.'

Rosa's progress up the social scale was aided by a sadly unimpor-
tant event in her life – an event which took place some months
before she started working for Margot Asquith. For on 13 June
1893 Rosa married. She married automatically, carelessly and
without love. She was twenty-five.

Excelsior Lewis was the twenty-nine-year-old butler to the
Honourable Sir Andrew Clarke, the son of an Irish landowner who
had risen to fame suppressing the Maoris, designing Australia's
political system, setting up a number of large naval arsenals and
fortifying India, amongst a number of other useful occupations.
Clarke had a cousin who was even more high-powered and was
indeed regarded by Victoria's court as an even greater fixer than
Lumley. Major-General Sir Stanley de Astel Calvert Clarke was a
member of the Marlborough House set and a close personal
friend of the Prince of Wales. He usually accompanied the Prince
on his innumerable journeys abroad and acted as a kind of
unofficial equerry. His closeness to the Prince made him even
more powerful than Lumley in the dirty tricks department, for
Lumley was more closely associated with Victoria than with
Edward. Nevertheless Clarke fully realized that Lumley had far
greater skill than he had at manipulation and he quite often
passed on problems that needed to be 'handled' to Lumley's
greater expertise.

Rosa's marriage to Excelsior Lewis seems to have been a
Clarke-and-Lumley operation. Amongst others, the Prince of

Wales had been for some time requiring a centrally placed suite of rooms where he could have sex and where the management was more than discreet. Rosa had been groomed by Lumley for just such a task but perhaps it was considered by Clarke that a husband would lend her an even greater aura of respectability – although there is no evidence to suggest that this was his idea. An arranged marriage was considered in the line of duty for royalty – not so for a servant. It may well have suited Rosa's ambitions to rise higher in status by these doubtful means, but it also affronted her instinctive sense of decency. She must, too, have felt a degree of self-contempt, for it was quite clear to her that ambition would triumph. So here was yet another reason for Rosa, at twenty-five, to become even more cynical – and even more determined to climb. She knew that she was being used, and indeed was as contemptuous of those who used her as she was of herself. But she sought a certain security from the Establishment of the times. After all, she was on her own and had completely renounced her own home and those belonging to it. She had always lived in, and basically regarded the shifting but secure environment of her employment as her home. Rosa was prepared to go through a marriage of convenience to Excelsior Lewis but in name only; she had no interest in him personally or sexually, although his later self-indulgences were to bring out a certain maternal streak in her.

The sham of their contrived marriage took place on 13 June 1893 at Trinity Church, St Marylebone. Excelsior was known to Rosa's family and was acceptable to them for the reason that he had saved a considerable nest-egg. They were, or course, unaware of the real motivation behind the marriage. It was Rosa's conventionality and sense of respectability that insisted on a church ceremony, although Excelsior had suggested that it should take place in a register office. In her usual flamboyant manner, Rosa afterwards related to Mary Lawton, 'I was working for Charlie Duff then, and I went off to Church, and we were married. I had nothing on but a common frock. ... I told the parson to be quick, and get it over ... So we were married' Then I threw the ring at him at the church door and left him flat ... I haven't lived with him yet, so I'm not really married to him yet.' In fact it's very unlikely that Rosa did or said anything of the kind, but these highly exaggerated anecdotes certainly spell out her frame of mind at the time – resentment, guilt and cynicism.

There were only three other people present – Edwin Hills, Rosa's younger sister Marianne, and an agent of the Establishment who was there to see all went well. The records at the church were deliberately falsified, Rosa giving her father's name as Edwin Ovenden rather than William Edwin Ovenden, and also claiming that he was dead. In fact the unfortunate man did not die until 1910. These lies were also countersigned by Marianne. Nor did Rosa give her address, merely writing 'Parish of Holy Trinity, Brompton'. What more could one add to these skeletal and devious nuptials except 'God Bless the Prince of Wales!'

At the time that colourful gentleman was conducting an affair in rented accommodation with the Marquise d'Hervey de St Denis. However, the premises were far from convenient as they were in Pembridge Gardens in Notting Hill Gate – which was definitely in the sticks. Now that Rosa was thoroughly set up, she could arrange a far more central house of convenience for his Royal Highness. In fact the premises, at 55 Eaton Terrace, just off Eaton Square, were registered under Excelsior's name, and the entry in the *London Directory*, for 1894 reads: 'Excelsior Lewis, 55 Eaton Terrace, S.W. Letter of Apartments'. The house was originally owned by a Miss Thynne, a member of the Marquess of Bath's family. It was now divided into two sections – living accommodation for Rosa and Excelsior, and 'lodgings'. Apart from front and back doors there was a private entrance that led from Chester Row through the back garden. The housekeeping budget was generous and four servants were maintained in the house, all of whom were handpicked for their discretion.

For a brief period Rosa did very little. The privilege of her position, the four servants, the coming and going of the celebrated clients, temporarily elated her. But once she became used to it, boredom set in. The sterile marriage didn't help, and Excelsior, far more affected by it than Rosa, began to drink. He was obviously aware of his pawn-like role, but was not intelligent enough, as his wife was, to use it to his advantage. His family, presumably not knowing his real role, also complained heavily that Excelsior was not cut out to be a glorified *concierge*. Indeed they claimed that if Rosa hadn't forced him to leave his orginal job he would now have every chance of eventually becoming a butler at the top of some great household.

To assuage boredom, Rosa bought a bicycle and rode aimlessly around London. But this was not to last – and neither was her under-employment. In fact the situation was really exploded by the arrival of Excelsior's sister Laura, who moved into Eaton Terrace to keep an eye on her now hard-drinking brother. Laura bitterly complained to Rosa about how badly she treated her husband and also pointed out that it was about time Rosa bore him a child. This, to Laura, was the solution to everything. It was not, however, any kind of solution to Rosa. She had no intention of having children – they wouldn't have fitted in with the scheme of things at all. So, she went out and started to cook on a freelance basis. This gradually became full-time work and Rosa was quickly in demand. Of marriage, Rosa said to Mary Lawton: 'Polishing the furniture, and keeping things clean all day. That's a nice piece of furniture – now let's go to bed – that's the average married life! You can't live that way – just eating and sleeping. It's not good enough! No, just stopping at home with my husband was not enough for me. I always wanted six or more to keep me company – and I feel that way to this day. I am very dependent on human beings and human atmosphere.' And as to children she told Mary Lawton: 'I didn't want any children either because I was always afraid of poverty – I had been so poor myself, and I knew all the misery of it. I did not feel I had time to have them. You see, I should expect so much of my children, and I should be so disappointed if they didn't come up to my expectations. I would rather have none. Successful people rarely have successful children, I've noticed.'

It seems hard to accept that Rosa was totally uninterested sexually. She was not a great beauty (Sargent's portrait flatters her absurdly) but as a young girl she had had a flawless complexion which stayed with her for the rest of her life. Her figure was good and she always dressed well and carefully. But it was her personality that made her really attractive to men. For she was gradually cultivating an image that she saw herself almost forced to play – that of the cheeky, raucous cockney sparrow. The fact that no such image existed in real life was of no importance to Rosa – but it was of the greatest importance to her clients, all of whom fondly imagined that the slum-dwellers they avoided in less fashionable parts of London had hearts of gold, abrasive wit and easily imitable tones. Rosa did all she could to back up this falsity, largely because she was now getting more and more desperate to retain identity. She was, in fact, considerably isolated. Having renounced her family, more or less renounced her husband, and being no longer an archetypal domestic servant, Rosa felt she was neither one thing nor the other. She was lonely, and it was not until she started outside catering and drew up her fleets of helpers that she began to be too busy to be afraid of her own isolation. Nevertheless she took the cockney-sparrow role with her to Marlborough House and other centres of high fashion – and gradually she became a character. For some time she was able to divorce her 'part' from her real personality. But after a while, as with an actress in a soap opera, the two personalities became uncomfortably mingled – and she was unable to separate entirely one from the other. 'Everybody clamoured for me', Rosa modestly told Mary Lawton. '. . . At one time, I didn't charge anything. Then I charged ten shillings a day; and then a pound. And so on up to the top of the tree. I used to go – when I first started catering – at six in the morning. In those days, I used to make the bread, the rolls, the salt sticks – buy everything and do everything in the house – for ten pounds or ten shillings – anything they liked to give me. I cooked because I loved to cook – the money didn't matter.'

In fact it mattered very much and Rosa certainly preferred ten pounds to ten shillings. She made them pay through the nose and as a result became an extremely wealthy woman. Most clients commented with awe on Mrs Lewis's expensive tastes in the culinary line, but few complained. Anyway, as Rosa realized, they could afford it!

Excelsior's reaction to Rosa's catering was one of extreme jealousy – and Laura's one of supportive criticism. This, of course, acted as a spur to her outside activities and she kept them company less and less. Over the next five years her free-lance catering business grew to enormous proportions until it became absolutely essential for every society hostess to have Mrs Lewis to cook for her. Meanwhile the 'business' at 55 Eaton Terrace continued, although it is true that Rosa was no longer around to further its discretion. However, this disobedience didn't draw any recorded reaction from Lumley or Clarke, so one has to assume that the assignations in the lodgings were proceeding smoothly in her absence.

Rosa equipped herself with a large catering staff – bevies of kitchen girls cum trainee girls who were all dressed alike in white with high-laced boots and chef's hats. She was conscious of the fact that she already had a very high reputation to live up to and free-lance catering of this kind, with all its difficulties, must in no way sour it. In fact she was determined to enhance her reputation. To do this she would be up in Covent Garden at 5 am to buy the very best vegetables and would then use the kitchen at 55 Eaton Terrace to prepare as many of the dishes as she could in advance. In the afternoon, Rosa and her entourage would descend on the relevant kitchen and the resident staff would bow out. It was during this period that Rosa met the only man she ever claimed really to love – and he was, in many ways, a very unlikely person to love.

Rosa Lewis first met Lord Ribblesdale when he asked her to supervise his kitchen regularly and to prepare dinners. Sargent also painted Ribblesdale's portrait and it now hangs in the Tate Gallery and is reproduced in this book. His aquiline, aristocratic features look almost malevolent and Sargent seems to catch, whether by accident or design, more than a hint of cruelty. Thomas Lister was the fourth and last Baron Ribblesdale of Gisburn Park. He was touchy, arrogant and had a highly explosive temperament which would often produce a scene, with the Baron losing all self-control. His daughter, Lady Wilson, wrote in a preface to her father's autobiographical work, *Impressions and Memories*, the following appraisal of his temperament:

'I have often wondered what sort of impression my father made on those he met for the first time. In spite of his good manners, he must have been alarming, although it is difficult to define why. Possibly we all feel a tremor before people and things we are not accustomed to, and I do not think one ever gets quite accustomed to him. His unexpected flashes of humour, his inexhaustible sympathy, his understanding of human frailties, came always as a surprise. A less pleasant surprise, however, was his quick temper. Storms of a violent description would come up out of the blue in a most disconcerting manner. I remember a particularly tempestuous episode, when he was seeing my eldest brother off to India, at Victoria Station. In the confusion of changing his railway carriage at the last moment, a great-coat of my brother's was left in the first compartment he had entered. My father claimed the coat, loudly and truculently from the occupants of the carriage, two dark-complexioned gentlemen smoking black cigars; they complied with his request with enthusiasm, throwing the coat out of the window with such a will that it knocked my father's top hat sideways. With a leap forward he was on the step of the train, and just about to blacken further the traveller's dusky eye, when the whistle blew, and he was pulled back on to the platform by the onlookers.'

It would be interesting to know what sort of action Ribblesdale would have taken if the occupants of the carriage had been white! Lady Wilson went on to say: 'Such scenes were easily provoked. In conversation he would do the same kind of thing. He would take exception to some statement, or disagree with some sentiment, and he would lose his self-control quite as quickly as his listeners would lose their nerve. Once the scud had blown over, however, the enchanting ripple of his wit would be resumed.'

I'm sure that was a great relief to everyone. However, in the bad-tempered Lord's defence, his background was a tragic one. The Prince of Wales nicknamed Ribblesdale 'The Ancestor', no doubt because of the brooding malevolence of his looks. But he had a good deal to brood about, as when he was only twenty-two, his father shot himself as a result of his gambling debts. Nevertheless, the real financial crash had come when the child was only four, when the impecunious third Lord Ribblesdale was forced to sell his horses, his house in Eaton Place and let out the ancestral home on a long lease. As a result Ribblesdale writes in his memoirs: '. . . my mother and we children – my sister Beatrix, my brother Martin and myself – had lived in and about London in small furnished houses in Chesham Street and Lowndes Street, and at Tunbridge Wells and Hampstead and Richmond, places much frequented by homeless or embarrassed gentle-folk.'

Perhaps it was this kind of life that soured him, coupled with his father's suicide. His mother was the dominant figure in his life and this was the vital link between him and Rosa. He needed maternalism far more than the average person; indeed, he never grew out of needing it. Rosa, of course, was able to supply it – because she needed to supply it. And she went on supplying it for many years.

Ribblesdale was also a frustrated artist – and had been from his boyhood. He had been born at the Hôtel de France in Fontaine-bleau, was perfectly bilingual and indeed seemed to have picked up a good deal of the French temperament. In 1892 he was appointed Master of the Queen's Buckhounds, an archaic office that had originated some six centuries before; later, from 1896 until 1907, he was the Liberal Whip in the House of Lords. By 1892, Gladstone was back in power and it was he who offered Ribblesdale the post of Master of the Buckhounds. The buck-hounds belonged to the Queen and being Master of them gave Ribblesdale the right to lead the royal procession up the course on the first day of Ascot.

On 4 August 1892, *The Times* had written gloomily: 'The majority of forty in the hands of a minister directing a mixed and unstable following in an ambitious and far-reaching policy would prove a precarious position hard to command.' Ribblesdale's mother, referring to *The Times*, wrote in her diary: 'It is to this policy that Tom is now going to commit himself. I find it difficult to follow his reasons for forsaking the Liberal Unionists who, I believe, represent the honest and moderate section of the great Liberal party.'

At the time, the Liberals were against all wasteful traditions, and there was no doubt in their minds that the buckhounds were not only a wasteful tradition but a very cruel one. Ribblesdale writes cynically in his memoirs: 'They (the buckhounds) cost the tax-payer money – hunting the carted deer was cruel – hunting generally was associated with Tory principles. It was kept up by grinding the faces of the poor, or at least breaking down their fences and cutting up their fields, and so on.'

Luckily for Ribblesdale and possibly for the buckhounds, Gladstone was not a man who liked changes, particularly when they had to do with tradition. Nevertheless the controversy continued for some time. Ribblesdale wrote: 'The battle of the Buckhounds raged during the whole of my three years of office, but thanks to the Queen and Mr Gladstone, we survived. The Queen, like Mr Gladstone, had always been used to them, and to having a Master of Buckhounds at her levees. Habit is ten times nature, so much so that she overlooked the fact that the Prince Consort never hunted with the Queen's Hounds, and held the heterodox view that red deer should be stalked with the rifle at the cost of much exertion.'

So that was that. Ribblesdale leased Englemere House, Ascot, to be nearer the buckhounds, and it was to these kitchens that he invited Rosa and it was here that she first began to know him. However, it is interesting to note that not one mention of her is made in Ribblesdale's memoirs, which were published in 1922 when the Cavendish was at its zenith. He was obviously too careful a man to be so indiscreet for he was later to spend years living at the Cavendish, knowing full well its reputation.

In Ribblesdale Rosa saw the ultimate to which she aspired. The French called him *'ce grand diable de milord anglais'* and this suited him, physically at least. It didn't, of course, give any indication how much *'ce grand diable'* needed mothering. Rosa regarded Ribblesdale through rose-tinted spectacles. Later she grew to know all his considerable faults. But she never lost affection for him. Afterwards, just as Rosa was enshrined as Lottie Crump in Waugh's *Vile Bodies* (much to her annoyance), Ribblesdale was taken by Shaw as the prototype for Professor Higgins in *Pygmalion*. Higgins was arrogant but his arrogance was based on a major lack of self-confidence – and Ribblesdale's own personality was not far away from that.

By 1897, Rosa was thirty and the most unusual, successful and socially acceptable caterer of the times. Meanwhile, one of her most enthusiastic clients was finding himself up to his neck in scandal, the worst having been the Tranby Croft affair back in 1890. This particular problem was something that Edward's public image only really recovered from when he became king some twelve years later. Already, in the previous year, Lord Arthur Somerset, a reasonably close personal friend of the Prince, had been found in a homosexual brothel, and Edward's own son, Albert Victor, was inevitably in some debauched situation that had to be hushed up. Tranby Croft, however, could be said to be *la crème de la crème*.

The house belonged to Arthur Wilson, a ship-owner, and the sporting Prince was there for the St Leger race meeting. Baccarat was played in the evening – a game that was illegal. During the course of the game, Wilson's son claimed that he saw Sir William Gordon-Cumming cheating. The next evening he claimed he saw him again, £225 accruing to Gordon-Cumming as a result of these manoeuvres. Five witnesses in all stated they had seen him and on 10 September he was charged with cheating by Colonel Owen Williams and Lord Coventry. Gordon-Cumming went indignantly to the Prince of Wales, who told him there was absolutely no point in denial. He then agreed to sign a document swearing he would never play cards again – a document that ensured the silence of everybody concerned. The Prince also put his name to the document. In 1891 rumours began and they increased in such strength that finally Gordon-Cumming decided to take court action. The Prince of Wales, abetted by his secretary, Francis Knollys, did everything he possibly could to keep the case out of court, by trying to get Gordon-Cumming before an army enquiry or an enquiry by the Guards' Club Committee. They failed. So once again the Prince of Wales was to appear in the witness box. He was severely cross-examined by Gordon-Cumming's solicitor, who accused him of playing an illegal game and breaking Article 42 of the Queen's Regulations, which specified that any dishonourable conduct by an officer and witnessed by a fellow officer must be reported to the culprit's commanding officer. Edward was, of course, a very senior army officer himself.

The Prince was under public scrutiny in court for over a week. He firmly stated that he had every confidence in Gordon-Cumming's accusers. As a result Gordon-Cumming lost the case, but the Prince lost enormous popularity. His mother, Victoria, gave him many homilies on self-reform; he was condemned by the Church, by the Kaiser and by the general public, as well as being heavily satirized by the European press. Much to the Prince's fury Gordon-Cumming, although expelled from more or less everywhere, including the army and his clubs, became something of a popular hero. He also married a wealthy American heiress shortly after the case, thus making himself an exceedingly rich man, even if he did have to live the life of an exile. But if he really cheated at cards, and it seems likely that he did, why? Gordon-Cumming was not a poor man and the sum he gained over the card table was comparatively small. The writer Michael Voysey, a friend of Rosa's just after the war, who has written a play on the Tranby Croft scandal, thinks that it was quite possible that Gordon-Cumming deliberately cheated for the hell of it, being bored and contemptuous of his company. That seems an interesting possibility and is supported by an old veteran of Edward's gaming parties who told Anita Leslie: 'Of course he cheated. We all did. It was such a nuisance being made to play and lose money, and I and a lot of the younger men longed to be dancing instead. But Cumming cheated *too much* and he had a lot of enemies.'

The Tranby Croft affair was followed, in the same year, by another divorce scandal, and the Prince continued to play baccarat. But despite the unpopularity resulting from Tranby Croft, the Diamond Jubilee of 1897 swung him back into favour again. The public sympathized with the sad figure of the aging Prince of Wales, waiting for a throne from which his mother refused to abdicate. They had also become used to his ways, respected his public dignity if not his private habits, liked the way he set fashion and behaved in a suitably élitist sporting manner. In fact the real point was that however arrogantly self-orientated the bored Prince may have been, the age would have been a damned sight duller without him.

The Prince, of course, had a wide circle of friends and they were certainly not all aristocratic. The American Paran Stevenses, for instance, hotel-owners in New York and Prince of Wales worshippers, descended on London society. The Prince liked Americans and patronized them, but was quite unable to persuade his mother to agree to the presentation of the Stevenses' daughter. To make up for this disappointment, the Prince threw a ball for her at Marlborough House. Minnie, the Stevenses' daughter, married Arthur Paget and later became a leading society hostess. Rosa, who worked for her, told Mary Lawton, 'She had most wonderful parties, and she didn't invite people – she used to *command* them by telephone to see her; so they had to come, anyhow.' As Lady Paget, Minnie Paran Stevens's beacon was obviously of penetrating social glare. Rosa said: 'Lady Paget's social career has never been equalled by any other American. Later on, she had a charming house in Belgrave Square and it was then that she had a terrible accident, which almost made her lame, and nearly ruined her life. She endured the most terrible suffering and the King used to go every day to see her when she was sick, and send her the most wonderful flowers and fruit.' There were other Americans moving in society at the time, known collectively and colloquially as 'the Prince's Virgins'. They were part of the Marlborough House set and preceded the social acceptability of the American male.

Two other important figures in Rosa's free-lance period were Sir William Eden and Waldorf Astor. Eden, who later stayed for many years at the Cavendish and had the most abrasive of all relationships with her, had an impressive list of titles. Apart from being a Count of the Holy Roman Empire, he was seventh holder of an English baronetcy and fifth holder of an American baronetcy. Like Ribblesdale he was an amateur painter, although of greater note and like Ribblesdale again he was a man of uncertain temperament. Margot Asquith remembered one incident which was typical of his personality. As Master of Foxhounds he was very conscious of keeping good relations with farmers: 'I saw him fling himself upon the floor when he was told that strangers had been seen riding across the newly-sown seeds of his favourite farmer.' Sir William resigned his commission as a lieutenant in the 28th Regiment of Foot when he married Sir William Grey's daughter in 1886, and from 1886 to 1896 he was Colonel commanding the 2nd Volunteer Battalion of the Durham Light Infantry. The similarities between Rosa's two most favoured men make clear her ideal prototype – an aggressive, arrogant, socially and physically powerful man, who was idiosyncratic and who needed a mother figure. Both Ribblesdale and Eden exactly answered this description.

William Waldorf Astor came in the wake of 'the Prince's virgins'. Astor was an American millionaire who was also an anglophile. He admired Rosa as a cook *par excellence,* partly because she was able to produce Southern American dishes – an art she had learnt while working for Willie Low. Later she was to produce celebrated meals at Hever Castle in Kent, Astor's bucolic country retreat. Waffles, sweet potatoes, huge water biscuits, peppercorns, Virginia hams, terrapin soup and brandy peaches were all on Rosa's American menu. And in gratitude Astor wrote to her saying: 'I thank Mrs Lewis for an excellent dish. [She had cooked him peppercorns]. I should be very glad if at her convenience she could give Mrs Reid a few lessons in the preparation of these American peppers, also the making of a consomme for my breakfast which at the office is very bad, an omelette and American corned beef hash.'

To show the sheer scale of the menus Rosa was asked to cook I have taken a few examples and reproduce them below.

EDWARD VII BUCKINGHAM PALACE
French President – Dinner 25 May 1908

Tortue Claire
Crème de Pois Comtesse

Blanchailles au Naturel et à la Diable
Suprêmes de Truites froides à l'Edward VII

Côtelettes de Cailles à la Carienne
Stewed white grapes

Selle d'Agneau à la Niçoise
Mousse de Jambon à la Fallières
Cold chicken cutlets
Russian Salad

Poussins rôtis
Ortolans sur Canapés
Salade à la Victoria

Asperges d'Argenteuil Sauce Mousseline

Chartreuse de Pêches à la Reine Alexandra
Grenadine de Patillierées

Oeufs de Pluvier
served with cream cheese

Soufflés Glacés à l'Entente Cordiale
Bonbonnières de Friandises

MRS JACOB ASTOR
30 Curzon Street.   24th June

Consommé aux Ailerons

Truite froide à l'Aurore

Cailles grillées Maréchale

Boeuf braisé en Bellevue

Jambon de Prague au Champagne

Poularde froide

Pêches d'Antigny

Pailles au Parmesan

LADY BRABOURNE
19 Curzon Street – Dinner for 21

Consommé Moevite

Truite Saumonée Sauce Hollandaise

Poularde   Soufflé froid

Selle d'Agneau

Cailles rôtis au cresson

Asperges

Fraises Melba

Biscuits glacés

Canapés au Parmesan

Normally, Rosa's luncheons were restricted to three courses – as a mere *apéritif* to dinner. But this rule was sometimes broken, as Lady Raglan describes in her *Memories of Three Reigns*: 'Our first dish was of grilled oysters and celery root on thin silver skewers, and then came one of those delicious quail puddings which are one of Mrs Lewis's inventions and for which King

Edward had a special liking. There was a whole quail under the paste cover for everyone at table. This was followed by a dish of chicken wings in breadcrumbs and kidneys, before the pears and pancakes, an admirable combination with which our lunch ended.'

During this period Rosa became an admirer and later friend of the Carlton chef, Escoffier. She told Mary Lawton, 'I consider Escoffier one of the greatest chefs of France, and one of the greatest in the world. He is the greatest gentleman among the bourgeoisie and one of the few Frenchmen I ever had any respect for.' Another example of Rosa Lewis at her tolerant best!

In December 1899 Rosa Lewis entered a new phase in her career – but a very temporary one. She was now thirty-two and had agreed to take on the catering at White's Club. Despite her glowing reputation, her appointment was not a wildly popular decision. Safe in their chauvinistic eyrie, some members resented a woman's presence, particularly when she brought in her 'girls' and a number of pet dogs. Undismayed by the vinegariness of these members, Rosa modernized the kitchen and then the menu. She told Mary Lawton, 'I went there to pull it together when it was taken over. I had never run a club before, and I ran the kitchen on the production of the dinners. Women didn't run the kitchens of clubs in those days – I am the only woman who ever did.'

The reason for her premature departure was a dispute over a quail. The snipe and quail were not expensive game birds but could be cooked with great imagination. One of Rosa's recipes for snipe was as follows: 'Take your cailles or snipe, and truss for braising, and leave in marinade for a few hours. Make an ordinary suet paste, line a basin with it, then place your quail or snipe, one for each person, in slices of beef as thin as paper, which when cooked dissolve into the sauce; put some fine, chopped mush-rooms, parsley, shallots and good stock, and put a paste top and boil for one hour. Serve rice or barley with it.'

Unfortunately, one of the members objected to the dish and confused Rosa's famous snipe with woodcock. A major row followed during which the testy member kicked one of her dogs – which shouldn't have been in the members' dining room anyway. As a result Rosa resigned and White's lost a very good cook. But whether they were so upset to lose her personality is another matter, for she was increasingly acting out the cockney sparrow image and this, unless enjoyed, could be both embarrassing and wearisome.

In January 1901 Queen Victoria died and the Prince of Wales at last became Edward VII. The next year Rosa began negotiations to buy the Cavendish Hotel. She had returned to free-lance catering after the White's debacle, and her culinary arts were as popular as ever – as were her talents for discretion.

THREE

The Cavendish

1902–9

'You see I really got the Kaiser through cooking for the King.'
ROSA LEWIS

EDWARD VII WAS CROWNED ON 9 AUGUST 1902. JUST AFTER his mother's death, in his extempore speech, he said, in reference to Victoria, 'My constant endeavour will be always devoted to walk in her footsteps ... I am fully determined to be a constitutional sovereign, in the strictest sense of the word, to work for the good and amelioration of my people.' In fact Edward had no intention of walking in his mother's footsteps, having already been living in her shadow for too long. Now she was dead he was anxious to make a good number of social changes. He did, however, keep to his promise to be a constitutional sovereign in every sense.

Very quickly the dusty conservatism of the Victorian age was over and with relief in came the hectic gaiety of the Edwardians. Edward was now in his sixties and was enjoying a greater vogue of popularity. In 1896 his horse Persimmon had won both the St Leger and the Derby, and he was 'good old Teddy' again. The shadows of the scandals dropped away, the age of dour Victorianism was at an end and everyone was looking to the new king to lift the mouldering lace blinds and let some sunshine in. This he had every intention of doing.

An emergency operation for appendicitis delayed the coronation, the first one for sixty-five years, but it finally took place on 9 August 1902. He began new-brooming almost at once by enlarging the court circle, redecorating Buckingham Palace and using it as his headquarters, appearing in public continuously and holding huge receptions with much champagne. Unlike his mother, he took no hand in affairs of state, but made sure that he dutifully attended a large number of public functions. Spring visits to Biarritz, and late summer visits to Marienbad continued, as did the usual round of racing, yachting, house parties, enormous meals and, of course, women. His popularity was now at a very high peak and the murky whispers of Tranby Croft, Mordaunt and so on went unheard. Edward had successfully lived down his past and was still womanizing. He really didn't deserve to get away with it!

Perhaps the secret of Edward's success was that he enjoyed being a king. After all, he had been groomed for it for sixty years and he had served a long enough apprenticeship. His programme of frantic gaiety was tiring and was eventually to kill him, but for the moment he was riding high – and Queen Alexandra was as long-suffering as usual. The writer Henry James privately considered him 'an arch-vulgarian' and in some ways James is right. Perhaps in most ways. But nevertheless, arch-vulgarity was just what the nation needed after so many years of Victorian arch-repression.

Around the time of Edward's coronation, Britain's popularity abroad was at an all-time low. The Boer War was in its last and messiest phase. 1899 had seen some particularly galling defeats for the British and now Kitchener was grimly failing to capture a number of guerrilla leaders who refused to surrender. Their hit-and-run tactics were very successful against the British army who were now facing humiliation after humiliation. As a result Kitchener burnt Boer homes, built thousands of block-houses, and confiscated produce and livestock from Boer farms, thus inviting an onrush of hostile criticism from both Europe and America. Britain was equally divided – as was the Government. So it was lucky for everyone that the country now had a King who was apolitical.

At the beginning of Edward's reign, imperialism was still at the peak it had reached by Victoria's Diamond Jubilee in 1897. Much of the world map was being painted red and a vast sum of money was being made and spent in the Empire. But a few miles from the hotel in Jermyn Street which Rosa Lewis was negotiating to buy, there existed some of the worst slums in Europe. Many missions existed in the East End, often involving the upper middle classes or the aristocracy. But education, soup kitchens and temperance lectures didn't really make up for lack of regular work, bad working conditions, and too little money for too many hours. There were the sweat shops too, which created appalling conditions. Despite this, the working class largely accepted their lot, were non-revolutionary and cheered Teddy on his public occasions – enthusiastically. One wonders, of course, what they would have made of his gargantuan breakfasts or his lobster teas or even his late-night snacks!

In contrast, the world of high society, like imperialism, was in its heyday. It was a golden age superficially, but in truth most people found it very exhausting, very expensive and, although they daren't admit it, motiveless and dull, despite the glamour. The Season was a particularly harrowing affair and many of its refugees ended up as the hard-drinking set in the Cavendish. Nevertheless, high society did allow a good deal of coy promiscuity and this is best epitomized in this extract from V. Sackville-West's famous novel, *The Edwardians*:

'The name of each guest would be neatly written on a card slipped into a tiny brass frame on the bedroom door. This question of the disposition of bedrooms always gave the duchess and her fellow-hostesses cause for anxious thought. It was so necessary to be tactful, and at the same time discreet. The professional Lothario would be furious if he found himself in a room surrounded by ladies who were all accompanied by their husbands. Tommy Brand, on one such occasion, had been known to leave the house on the Sunday morning – thank goodness, thought the duchess, that wasn't at Chevron! Romola Cheyne, who always neatly sized up everybody in a phrase – very illuminating and convenient – said that Tommy's motto was '*Chacun à sa Chacune*'. Then there were the recognized lovers to be considered; the duchess herself would have been greatly annoyed had she gone to stay at the same party as Harry Tremaine, only to find that he had been put at the other end of the house. (But she was getting tired of Harry Tremaine.) It was part of a good hostess's duty to see to such things: they must be made easy, though not too obvious. So she always planned the rooms carefully with Miss Wade, occasionally wondering whether that upright and virtuous virgin was ever struck by the recurrence of certain adjustments and coincidences.'

This extract also clarifies just what a full-time and nerve-racking job a hostess had – a job that became a nightmare when the king came to stay!

The atmosphere of the country house parties that Rosa catered for was uniquely Edwardian and could not have existed in any other era. Heavily formal, invariably trivial, the entire social ambience of these occasions was one of a great deal of social gloss, and a great deal of secret liaison. The enormous meals, the boredom of the light conversation, the 'above-it-all' interest in politics, the utter predictability of each hour spent was in itself exhausting. Rosa must have been startled by the rather over-exotic conversation of the ladies. 'Cheery' and 'ripping' were already established adjectives, whilst 'up-to-date' was just coming into its own. But other terminology was more esoteric: a tea-gown was known as a 'teagie', a royal personality known as a 'man-man' and divine was 'deevie'. The coy 'expie' meant expensive, the equally coy 'indie' meant indigestion and 'fittums' meant 'what a perfect fit'! It was essential that this language should at all times be observed and anyone who did not use it was definitely a social outcast.

It was not so bad for the men – at least they could escape to the hunting, shooting or fishing party. But it was appalling from the women's point of view, particularly as regards the dressing up, which could occur two or three times a day. Pads were inserted under the hair to provide the foundation on which the coiffure was built up, and it was, of course, essential that no hint of a pad should ever show. So inevitably, during conversation, many women were seized with the neurotic conviction that one such foundation was apparent and they were forever over-anxiously patting at their coiffures.

Their silk stockings were smoothed on by their personal maids and then the heavily boned long stays would be fitted over the chemise, fastened, and suspenders would be clipped to the stockings. Then lacing would be wound around the waist and elsewhere, pads would be fastened on the hips and under the arms so as to accentuate proportions and smallness of waist – and then madam's drawers would be hauled unceremoniously on. Then the petticoat, and then whatever dress milady eventually chose. It was a tortuous process and in the summer heat life must have been a perpetual misery, moving encased in a prison of quite primitive garments that were unyielding and unmerciful. Jewellery, of course, made up a little for the discomfort. But only a little. Like stately and close-hauled galleons the women paraded through endless days from breakfast in bed to luncheon in a room full of scattered tables and aimless conversation. Then on to intimate afternoon conversations (more pleasurable, and mainly gossip), to tea, to more dressing up, to dinner and then to bridge. The only high points in the day were the love passages, and these depended on the hostess's skill at room arrangement.

Meanwhile the service industry of these great, artificial households, the servants, continued an unabated daily round. They had their own pecking order, their own snobberies. Rank was the main obsession and this applied just as much to the outdoor servants as to the indoor – to the grooms, carpenters, glaziers, keepers, woodcutters, blacksmiths and tenant farmers. Hundreds slaved to ensure that the Edwardian household worked like clockwork, everything was provided to ensure that the greatest luxury prevailed. The smallest things mattered – at least in terms of Edwardian double-think. Prunes, to take a weird example, were never called prunes on a country-house table although for the kitchens they would be bought in a bag from the grocers and served in all their withered glory with custard. But in the dining room they appeared in a bottle, often labelled J.and C.Clark, Bordeaux, were known as French Plums and regarded as a great delicacy – and an anti-constipant. Needless to say they were never served stewed and it is not on record whether Rosa had a special way of dealing with them.

The social order of the kitchens was disrupted and disquieted by the appearance of Rosa and her team, and understandably she must have revelled in this. To be in such a dominant position, to be such a super-servant, boosted her confidence in the kitchens as much as in the heavily elegant rooms where she served her meals. The Sargent portraits, the deep carpets, the embossed notepaper – it was all a far cry from the Musgraves. Rosa fell in love with this vicarious society and although she was later to feel wounded by it, and later still to feel contempt for some of its members, she was never to appraise it properly. Perhaps one of the greatest and truest appraisals of Edwardian society appears in V.Sackville-West's *The Edwardians*, where Viola says to Margaret:

'The society you live in is composed of people who are both dissolute and prudent. They want to have their fun, and they want to keep their position. They glitter on the surface, but underneath the surface they are stupid – too stupid to recognize their own motives. They know only a limited number of things about themselves; that they need plenty of money, and that they must be seen in the right places, associated with the right people. In spite of their efforts to turn themselves into painted images, they remain human somewhere, and must indulge in love-affairs which sometimes are artificial, and sometimes inconveniently real. Whatever happens, the world must be served first. In spite of their brilliance, this creed necessarily makes them paltry and mean. Then they are envious, spiteful and mercenary; arrogant and cold. As for us, their children, they leave us in complete ignorance of life, passing onto us only the ideas they think we should hold, and treat us with the utmost ruthlessness if we fail to conform.'

And in later years it was these beautiful, spoilt, untutored, helpless children, equally hopeless as young adults, who would throng the rooms and corridors of the Cavendish, paying court to the reassuring figure of Rosa Lewis, the permanent, unchanging Edwardian, in an impermanent and changing world. For the rest of her life she was to be a cornerstone from an old world. An old world that was mercifully dead – yet had left its progeny to swim helplessly against the buffeting current of change.

Rosa's deciding factor in favour of buying the Cavendish was that it would give Excelsior employment as well as provide her with a bigger kitchen than the one available at Eaton Terrace. He and his sister Laura still presided over the original establishment, but there was little for them to do as the apartments, with the servants, ran themselves. Excelsior was still drinking heavily and was leading an aimless life, made more miserable by the fact that his marriage had now irretrievably broken down. If he *had* wanted a reconciliation, it would have been difficult, for the only place he could be sure of seeing Rosa was in the kitchen at Eaton Terrace during the mornings, when she was obviously extremely busy. And then she was surrounded by her disciple-like girls. Sometimes, of course, she would be away for days at a time cooking at some great country house. Excelsior must have had some feeling for Rosa, because he was almost obsessively jealous over her absences from his side, which were many, but it is very unclear what she felt for him. Certainly her views on men in general were highly critical, and as the years progressed she grew more cynical about them. At the same time Rosa had a vague, rough affection for Excelsior, largely based on pity or guilt over the 'arranged' marriage that had taken him so far out of his depth. To put him in as licensee of the Cavendish, and Laura with him, would certainly appease all concerned, particularly Excelsior's family who were consistent in their complaints about Rosa's wrecking of Excelsior's in-service career. This would solve everything – or so she hoped.

Rosa had, of course, already been associated with the Cavendish before she bought it, for it had a distinguished clientele and she had cooked for many of them. It is not clear whether Rosa was given 'permission' to change the arrangements at Eaton Terrace or indeed 'permission' to buy the Cavendish, but it seems likely that the decision gained approval. Rosa was still very discreet and assignations could be made as easily at the Cavendish as at Eaton Terrace. Edward, of course, could not take advantage of the arrangements, for he was determined to avoid further scandal and retain his constitutional image. His mistresses were still the biggest risk, but this risk he was prepared to take. But to meet them in the public limelight of the Cavendish would have been monarchial suicide. As far as Edward was concerned, Mrs Lewis had served her purpose.

The Cavendish had had a chequered career under a variety of names and in 1902 the lease was reassigned by the landlords to Excelsior Lewis. It had nine years to run: previously the lease had been held by Felipe Santiago Franco. Its address was 81 Jermyn Street and 21 Duke Street. There was no freehold as the property was part of the estate of Bethlem Hospital, which had gained a large number of buildings in the immediate vicinity in 1831, as a result of giving up land at Charing Cross which the Government wanted for use as an open space – now known as Trafalgar Square. The remaining years of the lease plus goodwill and fittings cost Rosa £5,000. At the time the rateable value of the building was assessed at £350, on which yearly rates had to be paid of £54 13s. 9d. The ground rent was very small and Rosa's annual rent and rates bill would be something in the region of £600.

Rosa's views on hotel keeping were typically forceful and she told Mary Lawton:

'I had never had a hotel before, and I had only been accustomed to very nice people with very nice houses, and I didn't like anything hotelly or cheap, or any servants who had ever been in a hotel. I trained all my servants myself. I wanted it to be like one's own home. I didn't want to have it like a hotel. I didn't want a lot of money. I like people, and I think if you make a place like the people you like, you get the people you like. You *attract* them. In the first place I don't like a lot of common pictures. I like clean linen, hot water and good food. I like things which can be washed and cleaned. Hot water, clean linen, and good food are the making of any hotel.'

It was unfortunate that Excelsior did not live up to Rosa's expectations and it was his mismanagement of the Cavendish that put the finishing touches to an already failed marriage. 'My husband didn't like me to go away. He was jealous – always thought I was in love with the people I cooked for . . . So I took the Cavendish Hotel, really for my husband . . .' She may have done, but she had absolutely no intention of living in it with him – at least not with Laura around. She much preferred to rent a small house nearby and live on her own. 'So I supplied my husband with chefs, and people for the hotel, and thought that, with the help of his sister I could go on living my life from my small house, and his sister could take care of him – feeling that she probably had more affection for him – and was more likely to make a go of him than me.'

Rosa deliberately blinkered herself to the impracticality of the arrangement and went on cooking. Excelsior went on drinking and when he wasn't drinking he was obsessively thinking about who his wife was sleeping with. Frankly he needn't have worried. Nevertheless, Excelsior's jealousy grew – and with it his drinking. Over the next nine months his mismanagement also grew and there seemed little his sister could do to help him. The previous goodwill of the hotel was fast being eroded, guests were leaving and tradesmen's bills were unpaid. Finally Rosa realized that she could no longer stand by and watch the Cavendish go bankrupt. She confronted Excelsior and to her horror discovered that the debts amounted to £5,000. Rosa caused a major scene before telling Excelsior and Laura to leave the hotel, which, after all, she owned. She described the scene to Mary Lawton but her account seems a little too colourful to be true and surely belongs to Rosa's 'cockney sparrow' identity projection, which she was now finding quite impossible to separate from her true self. 'I blackened my fingers from the chimney soot, and marked my face, to make it look as though he had assaulted me . . . I running round the table; running round with a cup of tea that I threw over him. Cups rattling and flying, a little disorder, a few black marks on my face . . . the cash-box stolen – couldn't be found! (Of course, knowing quite the right place to hide anything – being a cook – I had put it in the oven!)'

There was no need to have created the set-up for a divorce because in the end she never bothered to divorce Excelsior. There is no record of any proceedings and as she wasn't basically interested in marriage or children, she no doubt saw little need to bother with divorce. As to her financial problems, Rosa made Excelsior bankrupt and then 'took him out of his bankruptcy, paid twenty shillings in the pound to everybody he owed money to – also paying lawyers for both sides.'

With Excelsior and Laura gone, Rosa took over the hotel herself, aware that she would have to work off £5,000 in debts. The year was 1903 and the task before her seemed impossible. Yet there was no alternative. The only possibility was turning to her more influential friends for financial help and this she had too much pride to do. So, retaining only a few staff, she began to try to retrieve the fortunes of the Cavendish. Sixteen months later she had done it – and somehow physically survived. By running the hotel on a shoe-string, by continuing the outside catering service, by going to Covent Garden and pushing her bargains back on a hand-barrow, by buying quail at fourpence in the market and selling the birds to private customers at three shillings a head, and by bringing back 'left-over' game from country house shoots and selling that too, Rosa made a considerable sum of money. During this period her sleep was drastically limited and her meals practically non-existent. All this shows an extraordinary tenacity and single-mindedness – a sort of determined desperation that had been wrought out of her past experiences. In fact, this short period of Rosa's life was her best. She never responded well to success, and building-up situations were very much more her *métier*.

In 1903 Rosa leased the houses on either side of the Cavendish and also arranged with the Maudsley Trust to acquire another lease on land facing Mason's Yard. In 1904 she built a fourth wing, thus making a quadrangle which surrounded the gardens at the back of the original building. This achieved a private courtyard and garden and also ensured a greater intimacy in the atmosphere of the hotel.

Inside, Rosa furnished the Cavendish in the style of the big country houses in which she was used to cooking. She decided against a hotel atmosphere, realizing that as a growing legend she had every right – and need – to be exclusive. She wanted more of a club feeling to the buildings, and Rosa created this by turning sets of rooms into suites, each with their own private dining-room. One of these suites was earmarked for Edward VII but it is doubtful whether he made a great deal of use of it, particularly as he was trying to keep his sexual adventures in such low profile. A scurrilous comment in the *Sporting Times* ambiguously wrapped up the message that Edward had decided to make a change in his social habit:

> 'Queen Victoria's eldest son, while yet her heir, condescended or, with interest at Court, might be induced to grace the dinner-table of almost any millionaire or professional celebrity. King Edward VII visits his courtiers or his plutocrats at their country seats; but, save in cases wholly exceptional, he is not an evening guest at their London dwellings. Thus he shoots with Lord Burnham at Hall Barn, but he neither dines nor sups with him in Mayfair. This is a social note of the time, and is of good omen for the society I have called professional, in distinction to that which is merely smart.'

But despite Edward's decision to keep out of the limelight, Rosa was still asked to go and cook for him. She told Mary Lawton: 'When the King was invited anywhere, a list was submitted to him, or more or less to his first lady . . . [the mistress of the time rather than the long-suffering Queen Alexandra] and worked through her . . . The King's clique was always the same; . . . [bar the mistresses] . . . You knew just what rooms to put them into, and you knew just who was going to be at every dinner. Lady Randolph Churchill, Lord and Lady Savile, Lady Paget, Lord Chesterfield, Lord Kenyon, Lord Castlereagh and old Cassel.'

The furniture in the Cavendish was of the broad sofa and winged chair variety, and the panelled walls were painted white or dove grey. The public dining-room was added with the new wing and this became heavily patronized, for at the time there were few restaurants in London in which it would be deemed respectable to eat. So, in this club atmosphere, within a few minutes of Buckingham Palace, of the most fashionable shopping centre and of the most fashionable clubs (including the much despised White's), Rosa began to preside in an increasingly idiosyncratic manner. There were no bars as such and those wishing to drink would either do so in their private suites or would emerge publicly in Rosa's own parlour – a room which was to become notorious for heavy drinking, its seemingly endless supplies of champagne and its inevitable domination by Rosa.

As the Cavendish grew more and more fashionable, so the social order of the Edwardian era came into being. In particular the concept of womanhood changed and perhaps the most obvious manifestation of this was that it was now permissible to have far greater freedom. The Edwardian woman could now enter society as an individual rather than as one of a family party. Nevertheless, the *Queen Magazine* said admonishingly at the time:

'A bachelor who invites ladies to tea at his flat or luncheon on his yacht is careful to invite a relation also, or some married lady of a certain age, and does not consider two young married women without their husbands to be sufficient chaperons for each other from a critical point of view. An invitation to tea at a man's flat or at an hotel when given to only one lady is not a compliment to her. She is either too old to be attractive or too unconventional to need consideration on his part.'

Certainly the magazine was firm over the disastrous idea of an open affair with a man:

'Women should strenuously and fiercely cling to the con-
ventions and not overstep them for the sake of any man that
ever lived. To take only the commonsense view – nothing
higher – the strongest woman will find herself utterly alone,
while the partner of her indiscretion still has the *entrée* to his
friends and a place in society forever denied to her. In an
excess of magnificent, but misplaced, generosity, she may count
the world well lost, but he never will. She can never be sure of
him, for his friends, instead of deserting him as hers will have
deserted her, will do their level best to make him treat the
whole affair lightly and to assure him of their support and a
welcome when he chooses to break off the unwise connection.'

This feminine advice and cynicism about the man's 'getting
away with it' soon became out of date but for the first few years of
Edward's reign it definitely prevailed.

Many young debutantes naturally came to the Cavendish in its
early days, although there is no doubt that 'Mummy wouldn't
have liked it.' Rosa's circle had always been decadent and now her
hotel had become a flagship for the fashionable but racy. But the
girls were determined to go there just because of its doubtful
reputation. For despite the Victorian system of presentation at
court that Edward had preserved practically unaltered, the girls
were 'new women' and anxious to prove it. However, even with
greater conversational and social liberty, the Edwardian woman
did not have as much social conscience as her Victorian counter-
part. Charity was a moral duty to the Victorians and although
they blamed the poor for their plight they did not blame them as
much as the Edwardians did. They believed that poverty was the
result of idleness and improvidence and therefore coercion was
the only proper means of dealing with it. By 1905 one person in
six lived in a slum, and there were 14,470 paupers on the books of
the London unions. In fact the cost of pauperism, over the years
that Rosa bought and salvaged the Cavendish (1902–3), was
three and a half million pounds. *Queen Magazine* commented:

'Of course, this is far too high a proportion, but the noise
they make and the trouble they cause is largely in excess of their
numbers. However, it is chiefly for them that the rest of the
community has to provide policemen, workhouses and prisons,

and all the paraphernalia of repressive, remedial and philan-
thropic organizations ... Dramatic measures will be necessary
before the greater part of the evil can be stamped out.

In the first place, let it be accepted as an unbreakable rule
never to give money to beggars nor food or clothes to tramps.'

The sterilization of 'unfit' parents was often suggested and
Queen stated categorically, 'We cannot admit for a moment the
right of men and women to beget children when they have no
reasonable hope of supporting them.'

The answer to the working-class poverty problem – socialism –
induced instant paranoia in the Edwardian society. They accused
socialism, and specifically the Trade Unions, of creating poverty
by driving trade away with their greed. *Queen Magazine* said:
'One can have no sympathy with those of the working classes who
by their own actions, their greed, laziness, class selfishness and
unpatriotic behaviour have killed or driven away the trades that
supported them ... we feel bound to condemn the meretricious
and fallacious talk of the right to live or the right to work!'

But this was only a start, for as poverty increased the Edwardians
took an even harder line. They believed that failure or poverty
was the result of character weakness or defect. They also considered, with Samuel Smiles's popularization of the Victorian
liberal concept, that each individual was responsible for his own
spiritual and economic salvation. Finally they harshly believed it
was very unfair that the state should use taxes paid by hard-
working, successful, money-making people to subsidize the idle.
The *Queen* hotly cried, 'Why should the hard-working, thrifty
classes work the harder in order to support and continue a class
and system of which they disapprove?'

It was the survival of the fittest, combined with the extraordinary notion that owing to eugenics a poor or criminal parent
would produce a poor or criminal child because of heredity and
not because of environment.

So these were the extremes of attitude that existed when Rosa
Lewis was building up the Cavendish in the 'golden age' of
Edwardianism. Unintentionally, Rosa symbolized the working
classes hitting back. In other words, if you can't beat 'em, join
'em. And Rosa certainly joined.

As the Cavendish prospered in the short-lived reign of Edward, her two protégés, Lord Ribblesdale and Sir William Eden, were her closest friends amongst the clients. Sir William Eden, however, was not to become a real part of the Cavendish until after the King's death. Ribblesdale had now given up the position of Master of the Queen's Buckhounds, was now a trustee of both the National Gallery and the National Portrait Gallery and was also an Alderman of the London County Council. In 1903 he was sent to the States by the LCC as part of his duties as a member of a Royal Commission on London Traffic. He and Sir John Poynder sailed in great luxury on a Cunard liner (Ernest Cunard also had Rosa Lewis to cook for him) and once there they studied how the Americans were dealing with their own traffic problems. On his return, tragedy faced him when he received the news that his son Thomas had been killed in a battle with tribesmen in Somaliland. The date was 10 January 1904.

Ribblesdale had married Charlotte Tennant, whose sister was to become Margot Asquith. Ribblesdale was devoted to her – and indeed to his whole family of two sons and three daughters, the latter being known to the family as 'the dolls'. One of the dolls wrote of him: 'Although he was a lover of country life, he was very happy in London. His work was congenial to him, and filled his day with various interests. He liked to snatch a few days hunting or fishing; but I do not think, as he grew older, that he desired, or endured, long unbroken spells of the country.'

Lady Wilson, like her father, makes absolutely no mention anywhere of Rosa Lewis or the Cavendish. This doesn't mean that some sinister conclusion should be drawn, but it is clear from Ribblesdale's silence on the subject as well as his daughter's that the Cavendish was not considered a respectable place for his Lordship to haunt, nor Rosa Lewis a respectable hostess. Lady Wilson only says: 'He liked change of environment: it exhilarated him to leave the verdant desolation of a wet day in the country and, a few hours later, to feel the pavement of St James's under his feet and see the lights of Brooks's twinkling a welcome . . . Just as he loved change in his occupations, so he liked the diversity of the people around him. The originality of his mind, and his imagination, put him on terms of easy intercourse with all sorts and conditions of men.'

The death of Ribblesdale's son was a precurser of further tragedies to come and it was because of these, which took place over the next decade, that Ribblesdale changed from being an *habitué* of the Cavendish to a resident. An illustration of his very deep affection for his family is well illustrated by a letter he wrote to Charlotte, who was in Paris, in the heyday of his happiness. Dated 1896, it read:

> 'My dearest and ever dearest,
> Thank you very much for your dear birthday letter
> and for sending me the Millet. [A biography of the
> painter.] I am just going to have breaky with the
> Dolls which I do daily, and we try to add something
> to our little stock of poetry and hymns. I also try to
> read them the Bible stories you sent – a dear little
> book – but by this time I find it very difficult to fix
> their little attentions . . .'

Eight years later, in January 1904, Ribblesdale was reading the lesson at the funeral service of his son Thomas in the small country church on the family's estate at Gisburne.

Hardly a day passed without Rosa's cooking dinner for somebody. She was still a great perfectionist and inevitably unpopular with the regular domestic staff she and her girls replaced. Because of this she often used to disclaim her identity and pretend she was one of 'Mrs Lewis's assistant cooks'. She told Mary Lawton:

> 'This happened at Lady H—'s place, in Carlton Gardens. She, not being quite tip-top, all her stupid servants there didn't know me, and I had the greatest fun possible. And so they went on exclaiming about everything, and the butler said: "Oh, these lovely little truffles! These mushrooms! This is delicious! And this asparagus!" After each course of the dinner he would rush down and say nothing was ever so wonderful before, that *I* was very much better than the "great" Mrs Lewis, and had better stick to her, and then I could go all over the world.
>
> When the dinner was over he brought me down a bottle of champagne, which I handed to the people in the kitchen, having already refused the whiskey. The butler said, just as I was going out – "Oh, and who shall we tell her Ladyship to

send for?" "Well, you may tell her Ladyship to send for Jane!" said I, keeping it up to the end. The next morning Lady H— got on the telephone and said – "Mrs Lewis, can you send me Jane? I like her cooking so much!" She was going to give me £50. I was Jane, but I never let on.'

Although her language was always pretty foul, Rosa was so smartly dressed when she arrived at the great country houses that she was often taken for a guest. In fact she thoroughly enjoyed embarrassing her clients with this ruse and would spend hours laughing about it in the kitchens. Financially, Rosa was now very well off and during one season alone reckoned to make about £6,000 – an income quite separate from the one the hotel was already bringing her. By clever organization she managed to have at least five dinners going on in London each evening, the locations of which she visited on a rota basis. All the buying for these dinners was done by Rosa herself and many was the row she had with the tradesmen concerned. She would buy live quails at fourpence and tenpence each, she bought and killed her own turtles for her famous turtle soup, and she paid top prices for top-quality poultry.

A typical example of the bad relations between Rosa's staff and permanent staff occurred at a dinner party given by Lady Baird. When Rosa's head cook, Mrs Charlotte, arrived, Lady Baird's staff refused to cooperate and sat silently and sullenly in the scullery. The arrangement had been for the staff to help Mrs Charlotte, who was due to go on to organize another dinner. Somehow Rosa's staff coped, taking their revenge by using all Lady Baird's cooking and serving utensils instead of their own, so the recalcitrant staff were left with a large amount of washing up they hadn't expected.

Rosa cooked much of her dinner party food in the kitchens of the Cavendish, and then delivered her bounty in a hired bus. The entire operation was planned with military precision and she was more than impatient with anyone unable to come up to the same high professional standards as she set herself. She told Mary Lawton:

'If you are a professional you can have no excuses about hours, time, place or anything else, and I have always all my life avoided complaining about being tired, underpaid, inconvenienced or grumbling at my tools, for if you are a professional, you can never have a failure – you must keep all your troubles to yourself, and deliver the goods. No matter how great the inconvenience is, you can't let anything interfere with the success of your dinner. No matter what condition the kitchen you go to is in, you have got to make the best of it and let nothing interfere. Why! I would tear the leg off my drawers if necessary, any day, for a handle to a pot or an oven door and not grouse about it.'

During Coronation Year Rosa established her own all-time record by catering for twenty-nine supper balls in six weeks. As a result she received endless plaudits from her clients. Later she cooked at Sandringham and in 1908 received this handsome vote of thanks:

> 7 Carlton Gardens,
> St James's
> 30 May 1908

Dear Mrs Lewis,

I am sure you will be glad to hear that the Queen was so pleased with your dinner the other night that she sent Miss Knollys the next day to ask me for one of the Menus. I also had a letter from Lord Knollys to say the King thought it was an excellent dinner.

My brother-in-law Mr John Ward has taken Mrs Clark and two of my kitchen maids off my hands when I leave for Australia so she will remain on in this house which we have let to Mr Ward. I cannot spare her to him until the end of September when I leave, but he is going to Inver, the little Irish fishing lodge belonging to us, for his honeymoon about the 25th of June, and he wanted me to lend him Mrs Clark and one kitchen maid for a fortnight or three weeks up there. I cannot, however, do this so I am writing to ask you if you could find me a little plain cook and a kitchen maid on the job for him, to go out there and cook for himself and his wife for about three weeks? If you know of a suitable person the

best plan I think will be for you to send her round to
Mrs Clark who can tell her about the place and also
tell her how much in the way of dry stores she
would have to take up there with her. I should like
two girls whom you have trained yourself as Mr
Ward likes your cooking. Will you let me know
as soon as possible what you can do? She would have
to go to Ireland on the 24th of June. The fishing
lodge is in Connemara and Mrs Clark can give you
all particulars. Mr and Mrs John Ward would be
alone there.

Thank you so much for all the trouble you took
for me for my two dinners and parties the other
nights.

Yours faithfully,
[Lady] Rachel Dudley

In June 1907 Lord Kenyon, Edward's equerry, proposed a
grand lunch for Edward and Alexandra to be held in the Guildhall
in Bangor, North Wales. Kenyon wrote to Rosa asking her if she
would cook the meal.

The Albany
Piccadilly, W.
3 June 1907

Dear Mrs Lewis,

I shall probably have to give a luncheon to the
King and Queen on the 9th of July at Bangor,
N. Wales. Could you come and cook it for me? Don't
say anything about it. There will probably be about
50 guests if I can get them into the room. If you are
free let me know and I'll come and talk over details
with you.

Yours truly,
[Lord] Kenyon

Rosa and her team cooked the food in London the day before
the luncheon, and took it to Bangor by the midnight train. There
were no kitchens in the building, and as the place was locked up
when they arrived in the early hours of the morning, Rosa and her
cooks had to make an undignified entrance through the window.

The streets were packed as the King and Queen drove to Rosa's lunch, waiters came in from miles around and the food was served on gold plate. There were over ninety guests and the occasion – and the menu – was a great success. As a result Kenyon wrote this letter of thanks to Rosa.

> The Albany
> Piccadilly, W.
> 13 June 1907

My dear Mrs Lewis,

I was sorry not to be able to see you on Tuesday after the luncheon. Everything was perfect and I have been smothered with congratulations so that I begin to feel that I cooked it myself.

I send you a small souvenir of the occasion. The date on the buckle is so small that I can hardly read it, but it is there.

> Yours truly,
> [Lord] Kenyon

It must have been her finest hour.

At this time Rosa was a kind and compassionate employer, as was witnessed by Violet Drury who joined the kitchen staff in a lowly position in 1911. Violet was nineteen and was the daughter of the stud groom to William Macylow at Wellsbourne House. Rosa often used to cook for dinner parties there and this is how she met the young Violet. Violet's sister, Ethel, used to visit her in the kitchens when she was fourteen, and she vividly remembers Rosa's going about her daily routine with enormous efficiency and calmness. Ethel remembers the kitchens as being very old-fashioned indeed but nevertheless culinary miracles were produced from them. Violet stayed in the hotel kitchens until she became Head Woman, which appears to have been a logistical post which had nothing to do with the actual preparation of the meals.

The next important association Rosa had was with the Kaiser. She worked for him at a time when relations between the Kaiser and the Prince of Wales were heavily strained. Not that they had ever been very good. Frederick III's very short reign ended in 1888 and as a result Victoria's most beloved grandchild came to the German throne. Predictably, Edward detested his nephew and they had quarrelled well before William became Kaiser. Edward had given his support to a love affair between the German Princess Victoria and the Crown Prince of Bulgaria – a match that was condemned by William I, who was Kaiser then, and by the Kaiser-to-be, William II, Edward's unloved nephew. Edward had interfered elsewhere in German affairs, probably deliberately, and William had forbidden his uncle's attendance at Austrian army manoeuvres. The quarrel dragged on and, as Keith Middlemas says, 'Uncle and nephew were contrasting and jarring personalities; the one hedonistic, but controlled and diplomatic, the other flamboyant, arrogantly conscious of himself as the supreme representative of the German people.'

William admired the English monarchial system, although he certainly didn't admire Edward. He was also almost obsessively fond of Britain and his regular appearances at Cowes always managed to irritate Edward considerably, particularly as the German yachts often won. In fact it put Edward off the sport, so unbearable did he find the personality and company of his anglophile nephew.

However, in public Edward's self-control remained rigid and he was openly courteous to the Kaiser. It is only in his own personal correspondence that he damns him almost apoplectically. In 1884 he had given him the position of Colonel in the British Army, but this only gave William the right to meddle in the early years of the Boer War. What Edward found really insurmountable was William's priggish condemnation of his more notorious activities as Prince of Wales. He was furious when William failed to prevent the German press from satirizing him after the Tranby Croft disaster, when a cartoon appeared changing the motto of the Prince of Wales from '*Ich Dien*' to 'I deal'.

In 1901 Edward had made two visits to Germany, both of which were overshadowed by the failing Victoria. Edward was anxious to maintain good Anglo-German relations but once again he found it impossible to maintain good relations with the arrogant William. This still seemed a pity to Edward, for William had spoken in early January of an alliance between two 'Teutonic nations', pointing out that European peace might well be secured by the strength of German arms and the equal strength of the British navy. But good relations were not to be and the Kaiser was given a somewhat frigid reception at Sandringham. Edward was still anxious to come to terms with Germany, but at the same time Chamberlain was sowing the seeds of friendship with France. In 1905 the Kaiser again criticized British foreign policy and the Tsar, offended by Britain's ties with Japan and annoyed by Edward's political journeyings, called him 'the greatest mischief-maker and the most deceitful and dangerous intriguer in the world'. William agreed.

By 1907, the relationship between Edward and William was very tense and his next visit was not spent at Sandringham – or in any other royal palace. Edward excused himself on the grounds that the King and Queen of Spain, the Queen of Portugal, the Queen of Norway and the Empress of Germany would all be in the country at the same time as William – and there would not be enough accommodation to house this embarrassment of royalty. Therefore William rented Highcliffe Castle in Christchurch, Hampshire. He was not necessarily reluctant to do this, as it was one of the show-place stately homes of England and he knew, with true German thoroughness and efficiency, that he could just about cram into it his retinue of some ninety people – all transferred direct from the German royal yacht. Highcliffe belonged to a distinguished British soldier, Major-General the Hon. Edward James Montagu-Stuart-Wortley, and the Kaiser, who admired the British army, found his landlord more than acceptable. Rosa had cooked for Wortley and therefore it was natural for him to suggest to the Kaiser that he too should acquire the services of Britain's premier cook.

Rosa moved into Highcliffe and began the monumental task of arranging the catering for a crammed house of over ninety Germans. Stocks of food swiftly ran out locally, and so Rosa travelled to London every night on the royal train to replenish the stores.

Rosa was able to observe closely the Kaiser's personal habits when he was there and she found him a likeable man. She admired his efficiency above anything, the way he ran the crowded house so successfully. She noticed that he ate with special cutlery because of a withered arm and that he didn't want to be served with birds or fish with small bones which were difficult to handle with his disability. He ate game, ham, and a large amount of fruit. His punctuality at meal times (and everywhere else) also appealed to Rosa – as did his very obvious enthusiasm for her cooking.

But Rosa didn't just confine her activities to Highcliffe. She went with the Kaiser on his visits to the English aristocracy, taking over the kitchen of each house as he dined there. She was also invited to dine on the royal Yacht (she didn't think much of the food!), and as a reward for her culinary services William gave her a decoration (promptly returned at the start of the First World War) and a brooch, which she kept. Rosa told Mary Lawton: 'Eulenberg was with the Kaiser at Highcliffe Castle. He was more than a secretary; he was a very big person; very high up; next to the Emperor. I must say I felt that all the people with the Kaiser really cared for him . . . I have got a lot of the Kaiser's menus and things. I used to write out the menus for the day in my own handwriting and send them to him every morning. The menus were really the most difficult, because the Kaiser would only have them written in German or English.' It is certainly unlikely that he would have wanted them written in French in the current diplomatic circumstances – even if Rosa's gourmet-style French did make the language seem more attractive! 'The Germans', she continued to Mary Lawton, 'are certainly very easy people to cater for, because they are so methodical about everything they do – even their pleasures.'

Politically the outcome of the visit was not good and Rosa's cooking failed to seduce the Kaiser into a less irritable mood. Just after the state visit to Windsor, William blandly announced that he would be extending the German navy! He was now convinced that his uncle was anxious to destroy him and his country, and he publicly stated that the British monarch was not desirous of peace but instead 'aimed at war'. Paranoiacally he saw Edward as the master-mind behind every anti-German event, feeling or influence. This was far from being the case, for Edward was still anxious for appeasement and public concord. In private he abhorred William and it was unfortunate that William was not able to be equally discreet, for he was very public over his denunciations of his uncle. It was this clash of personality that made every diplomatic move doomed to failure although no one suspected, or imagined in their wildest dreams, the dark horrors of what was to be the bloodiest war in history. Soon the Kaiser, who had so regally stayed at Highcliffe and relishèd Rosa Lewis's imaginative cooking, was to be recast in the role of devil incarnate and parodied with the same savagery as his later and more demonic successor, Hitler.

FOUR

Accolades
1909–14

'He [Sir William Eden] used always to write when he was coming
from abroad, giving me various stiff orders about his wants on
his arrival, and say he would be quite glad to see my nice cheerful
face, and hear my bad language again.'

ROSA LEWIS

BY 1909 ROSA WAS FORTY-TWO AND HAD MORE THAN MADE her name. Not only was she celebrated in court circles, in aristo-cratic circles, in upper middle-class circles and in fashionable American circles, she was also now acceptable in political circles – particularly after her Highcliffe period. She had now become a celebrated public figure, was much (but only respectably) dis-cussed in the Edwardian press and was revelling in it. Fame gave her the confidence to be more outspoken, more idiosyncratic. She knew that the 'cockney sparrow' image was now an integral part of her success and was worth as much to her as her cooking and organizational abilities.

In February of the same year, the *Daily Telegraph* reported:

FOREIGN OFFICE DINNER
WOMAN COOK'S TRIUMPH

'Ministerial banquets on the eve of the opening of Parlia-ment or in celebration of the King's birthday possesses an interest for the ordinary mortal distinct and apart from the dinners, however important, that are given on other occasions. The careful housewife is wont to wonder what are the resources of a great Government department to serve a well-chosen dinner of the conventional succession of courses, and whether or not more wonderful dishes often figure in the menu. Of course, in very many instances the Minister who is giving the banquet simply calls in one of the leading firms of caterers and has no further responsibility in the matter until the bill is sent in. At the Foreign Office, however, the system in recent years has been different, and on Monday night, when Lord Crewe gave his full dress dinner, as in 1908, all the arrangements were undertaken by Mrs Lewis, the well-known cook, who is not only proprietress of the Cavendish Hotel, Jermyn Street, but is called into the most exclusive houses in London, when the dinner or ball-supper is to be something quite exceptional.'

To give an idea of the bombastic Edwardian meals Rosa was still preparing, here are two more typical menus. The first is the story of everyday cooking at the Cavendish, and the second is typical of the kind of menu she produced for the Astors at Hever Castle.

CAVENDISH HOTEL
Dîner du 26 Juin, 1908

Consommé aux Ailerons
Truite foide à la Cavendish
Blanchailles
Soufflé de Cailles à la Valencienne
Pièce de Boeuf à la gelée en Bellevue
Jambon de Prague aux fèves
Poularde froide à la Parisienne
Salade
Asperges en branches
Pêches à la Marron
Bombe glacée Dame Blanche
Friandises
Laitances à la diable

HEVER CASTLE
Dîner du 10 Juillet, 1909

Melon Glacé
Consommé Princesse
Bisque d'Écrevisses
Blanchailles
Suprême de Volaille à la Maréchale
Selle d'Agneau à la Chivry
Foie Gras à la Gelée
Salade Nantaise
Cailles rotis sur canapés
Pêches Rosa de Mai
Caroline Glacées
Croûtes de Merluche

Edward would have approved of both menus. They were imaginative, well presented and – well, filling. The mind boggles at how long they must have taken to eat, how many wines went with each course, and the resulting cholesterol count. Owing to the wealth of her clients, Rosa did not spare expense or ingredients or trimmings. In fact, she was hideously expensive, produced a good deal of wastage (which she removed for her own private transactions) and was still held in intense jealousy by the resident cooks and staff from whom she and her girls took over. The Lewis entourage was blamed for everything by those regularly below stairs, from breakages to waste and from missing items to disruption. Some of the criticism was justified, other aspects of it were the patent results of the regular kitchen staff's being made to feel grossly inferior on important occasions – an inferiority which Rosa was not likely to bolster up.

Rosa, now publicly famous as a cook, began to publish her recipes in the *Daily Mail* and one such article, which appeared on 25 February 1909, read:

'For quail or snipe soufflé you make first of all a very good soufflé of any kind of game. Faisan or chicken for quail soufflés, the same will answer for snipe or woodcock.

Line your soufflé dish with the prepared soufflé, take your cailles, remove the neck bones and fill in with fine braised vegetables, what is generally known as Brunoise. Then place the quails in the soufflé having made a very good gravy with the bones.

Then fill up the soufflé with the mixture and steam for one hour very slowly.'

Further on the article read:

' "You can cook the most delightful things on a grill," Mrs Lewis explained. "Nothing can be better than grilled soles, for instance. A shoulder of lamb never tastes better than when grilled. You can grill turbot better than you can boil it. Grilled chicken is delicious . . . In fact you can grill anything, any kind of fish, meat or bird! The grill is *the* thing, and Englishwomen should give it the place on honour in their kitchen." '

The Cavendish clientele, meanwhile, became more and more celebrated. Eden and Ribblesdale had not as yet taken up residence, but the old, rambling rooms of the hotel were humming with gossip and intrigue, and a kind of romantic tattiness filled the atmosphere. Although the King was anxious not to frequent the bedrooms of the Cavendish, Hilaire Beloc's lines about the traditional Edwardian house-party seem to typify an atmosphere in the Cavendish that was to linger there well after the Edwardian era was gone. In fact it lingered right up until the builders moved in to demolish the buildings in 1962. Belloc wrote:

> There will be bridge and booze 'till after three
> And, after that, a lot of them will grope
> Along the corridors in *robes de nuit*,
> Pyjamas, or some other kind of dope.
> A sturdy matron will be sent to cope
> With Lord —, who isn't quite the thing,
> And give his wife the leisure to elope,
> And Mrs James will entertain the King!
>
> *Envoi*
> Prince, Father Vaughan will entertain the Pope,
> And you will entertain the Jews at Tring,
> And I will entertain the larger hope,
> And Mrs James will entertain the King.

Indeed the Cavendish, designed like an old country-house, epitomized the Edwardian house-party in full swing all the time – a demonic, exhausting *huis clos* type of situation. Add to this the aura of the novels of Elinor Glyn and its exact atmosphere can be conveyed. Mrs Glyn's five-million-seller *Three Weeks* was unique in appealing to women both below stairs and above. Published in 1908, its torrid story centred around a Balkan queen who was in the habit of receiving her lovers lying on a tiger skin and dressed in loose-fitting garments. So great was the success of the book that its rather humourless author was invited to stay at the Court of St Petersburg to write up a similar theme in Imperial Russia. Lord Curzon went with her as her escort. In her book, *Edwardians in Love*, Anita Leslie writes: 'I myself will never forget reading the forbidden *Three Weeks* which I found in a guest room when I was about fourteen years old – I thought it was true! And although we did not actually understand what went on in the Cavendish, my young brother and I felt the atmosphere of mystery and intrigue as we explored the long creaky corridors and peered into the bedrooms hung with chintz and sporting prints and huge gold mirrors. We thought it a house unlike any other in the world, and this childish assessment was perfectly accurate.'

Rosa opened the Elinor Glyn room for 'private' functions and she furnished it in the most seductive style she could. She wanted to create the aura of Glyn's novelettish work, although the renowned lady never actually visited the Cavendish. The walls of the room were panelled in white, there was an Adam chimney-piece and the furniture was either Sheraton or Hepplewhite. A huge sofa was one of the room's chief features. This was covered with a glazed mauve chintz and dozens of cushions were piled high on it. As a love nest it would appear to have been highly dangerous, suffocation rather than copulation being the most likely thing to be achieved. Later the room was to fall into sinister decay and in the dim, dusty twilight of its later years, Rosa, sitting downstairs in her famous parlour, sipping champagne and uttering imprecation or anecdote, must have fancied she heard its dulled ghosts up there carrying on with their everlasting house-party.

The following description of the real-life Lady Brooke is typical of the style of the famous Glyn writing and also makes it clear how wide-ranging her readership was, allowing for the narrow sexual views of the time.

'No one who ever stayed at Easton Place ever forgot their hostess, and most of the men fell helplessly in love with her. In my long life, spent in so many different countries, and during which I have seen most of the beautiful and famous women of the world, from film stars to Queens, I have never seen one who was so fascinating as Daisy Brooke. She would sail in from her own wing, carrying her piping bull-finch, her lovely eyes smiling with the merry innocent expression of a Persian kitten, that has just angled a ball of silk. Hers was that supreme personal charm which I later described as "It" because it is quite indefinable, and does not depend upon beauty or wit, although she possessed both in the highest degree. She was never jealous or spiteful to other women, and if she liked you she was the truest most understanding friend.'

It is not on record whether she liked Elinor Glyn! Glyn also found the Edwardian house-party sexual *frisson* rather fun: 'It might be a lovely lady's own lover who was sitting beside her, but he would never lean on her or touch her arms to accentuate his speech, for all touching in public was taboo.'

One wonders what Elinor Glyn would have made of a present-day encounter group, or indeed how she would fit into one.

Meanwhile the Cavendish continued to be a highly fashionable place with a long list of distinguished guests. Amongst these were the Grand Duke and Duchess of Hesse who used to come regularly every two years until the outbreak of the First World War. The arrangements were made with true German thoroughness, as epitomized in the following two letters:

ROYAL CRESCENT HOTEL

Filey, 8 July 1910

To the Cavendish Hotel,
London.

Their Royal Highnesses the Grand Duke and Grand Duchess of Hesse intend to come to London on July 15, in the evening for about five days or a week. Would you let me know if you should have room for them and what the terms should be?

They should require:

1 bedroom for Their Royal Highnesses,
1 dressing-room for His Royal Highness,
1 bedroom for Baroness Rossmann,
1 bedroom for myself,
1 sitting-room for meals as in 1908,
Bedrooms for each of the servants (two male
    servants and two maids).

We should have breakfast in the morning always in the hotel, the other meals not regularly. The servants would have all meals at the hotel.

Arrival in London not before 6.15 pm.

I would be much obliged by an early answer and also if you could recommend another hotel in your neighbourhood in case you are not able to give us rooms.

F. Massenbach, A.D.C.

GROSZHERZOGLICHE GENERAL-UDJUTANTUR
Darmstadt

Dear Mrs Lewis,

Many thanks for telegram and letter. I forgot to say that we should like to have breakfast at our arrival on Tuesday morning. H.R. Highness takes coffee and I tea.

Yours faithfully,
F. Massenbach

Inexorably the freneticism of the Edwardian era pounded on. Rosa became interested in polo and regularly visited Hurlingham and Ranelagh, no doubt cheering on her favoured Cavendish-orientated team in a manner which some of them may have regretted. She bought the leases of Nos. 82 and 83 Jermyn Street, thereby providing annexes to the original buildings. She trebled the size of the kitchens, and furthered her own legend by asking her more favoured clients to sign a pair of her own corsets as a kind of autograph book. It is not clear whether Edward added his own signature, as popular rumour would have it, but it seems unlikely that he would be quite so indiscreet – particularly when he thought of what the Kaiser might say!

One of the greatest and one of the last of the Edwardian practical jokers was Horace de Vere Cole, first husband of Mavis de Vere Cole, who was later to become almost as close to Rosa as Daphne Fielding. Rosa also valued Horace de Vere Cole as a client and very much relished his grand-scale jokes. An old Etonian and brother-in-law of Neville Chamberlain, de Vere Cole became renowned for his hoaxes. Disguised as the uncle of the Sultan of Zanzibar he had enjoyed an official reception at Cambridge, and as 'Emperor of Abyssinia', with his suite (which included Virginia Woolf and Duncan Grant) he had graciously received another official reception, this time on board HMS *Dreadnought* at Weymouth. Amongst his other gems was haranguing a group of workmen who were under the impression that he was Ramsay MacDonald. He also dressed himself as a workman and began to dig up part of Piccadilly. He then returned, re-disguised as a disgruntled member of the public, demanding to know what was going on. Disguised as the Anglican Bishop of Madras, he confirmed several boys at a public school. He also walked past a policeman with what appeared to be his penis hanging out of his trousers. When just about to be accosted, he produced a pair of scissors and snipped off the 'penis', which turned out to be part of a cow's udder. Other star turns included sitting on the pavement trying to sell Augustus John paintings with little financial result and the famous story of his slow taxi-ride around Piccadilly with Sir Shane Leslie. Making sure that the taxi was as near to a policeman as possible, de Vere Cole opened the door and flourished the dummy of a near-nude woman. Banging the head of the dummy hard on the roadway, he shrieked out 'Ungrateful hussy'!, dragged it in again and told the taxi-driver to 'drive like hell'.

Never malicious, the pranking Cole played at least one kind of joke each day, and claimed, just before he died, that he had perpetrated over a hundred hoaxes.

After a brief Army career, he went to Trinity, Cambridge, and then was asked to enter Parliament, but refused. He wrote of himself: 'Played many jokes which the (in my opinion) greatest living Irishman said would live longer than any other affair of our time . . . I have travelled in the Sahara as a deaf and dumb Arab and got away with it. I have played and got away with more jokes than any man ever has . . . A great living artist said once, "Women are bloody bitches, you can't expect them to laugh at Horace's jokes – but a man who doesn't see the humour in them must be a bugger".'

Like Mrs Lewis, de Vere Cole was also a snob of the highest order. Wealthy, but financially imprudent and a disastrous investor, de Vere Cole was deep in debt by the 1930s and had already divorced his first wife. He made a list of the property he had owned (and presumably speculated away) and this was as impressive as his manic desire to amuse – although whether it was to amuse himself or others has never been quite clear. The list read:

House 43 rooms (without kitchens etc.) W.C.s 8 !

Corridors 6   Kitchens 2   Cellars 7   (over 18,000 bottles
   and 2,500 champagne)
1 London House (6 Chesham Street)
Rented – 34 Cheyne Row and 86 Cadogan Place
14 Estate Houses
1 Church

He married Mavis on 31 January 1931 and the papers commented that 'Mr de Vere Cole proves he is not joking this time'. He was one of the last in a long line of genuine Edwardian eccentrics, and his surreal activities provided not only a great source of amusement to Rosa Lewis but also a special flavour of Edwardian high-life that she was to cling to herself for many years afterwards.

In 1910, to Rosa's great distress, King Edward died. He was sixty-nine and Rosa forty-three. Edward's health had been failing since 1905. He had sustained leg injuries, one caused by tripping over a rabbit hole in Windsor Park, and the other on Sir Thomas Lipton's yacht. But the main trouble was his self-indulgent style of living and an increasing number of bronchial attacks. These were not helped by Edward's insistence on continuing to smoke considerable numbers of cigarettes and cigars each day. He had already publicly collapsed in 1909 during his state visit to Berlin and he went as usual to Biarritz for the 'cure' in 1910. But even this great resort and its psychosomatic healing properties could not compete with so many years of gargantuan breakfasts, lobster teas, huge dinners, little snacks, cigarettes, cigars, wine, brandy, liqueurs, spirits and the whole vast catalogue of human self-indulgence.

Back home again, he insisted on inspecting the planting of some crops in the pouring rain and in early May he had a severe bronchial attack. By the 4th of May Edward realized that he was up against the possibility of death, although he was determined to fight. On the 5th of May he gave his last official audience, Queen Alexandra hurried back from Corfu, and the entire royal family assembled at Buckingham Palace – an event that the dying King could only look on as a premature wake. Edward told them he felt 'better' and reaffirmed his intention of fighting back. One or two other officials saw him and realized that there was little chance of recovery. In the afternoon of the 6th of May he collapsed and suffered a number of heart attacks. It was at this point that Queen Alexandra made her most magnanimous and loving gesture. She invited Mrs Keppel to be amongst their mutual friends who had come to surround Edward as he died.

Mrs Keppel occupied a unique position amongst the many women that Edward loved. In today's world she would fulfil the role of a very super personal assistant to a highly chauvinistic employer. She was a friend of the celebrated Agnes Keyser who also, during a middle-age rendered unmarried by her dedication to nursing, gave her friendship and affections to Edward. Agnes Keyser, however, was forty-six when she first met Edward in 1898 while Alice Keppel was twenty-nine and very beautiful. For the next twelve years Edward depended on Alice Keppel for his every whim – with occasional reversions to Agnes Keyser who acted as a kind of 'drier-out', 'nursemaid' and 'health advisor'. But it was Alice Keppel who had everything else – except Edward's deep affection for Alexandra and his family. Mrs Keppel's husband raised no objection to her royal liaison, and she became Edward's constant companion. She also, very surprisingly, became a friend of Queen Alexandra and she and her husband often stayed at Sandringham. A good summary of her personality is to be found in the private file of Lord Hardinge of Penshurst, then head of the Foreign Office. (It was later published in the *Life of Edward VII* by Sir Philip Magnus.) He wrote:

'I used to see a great deal of Mrs Keppel at that time, and I was aware that she had knowledge of what was going on in the political world. I would like here to pay a tribute to her wonderful discretion and to the excellent influence which she always exercised upon the King. She never utilized her knowledge to her own advantage, or that of her friends; and I never heard her repeat an unkind word of anybody. There were one or two occasions when the King was in disagreement with the Foreign Office, and I was able, through her, to advise the King with a view to the policy of the government being accepted. She was very loyal to the King, and patriotic at the same time. It would have been difficult to find any other lady who would have fitted the part of friend to King Edward, with the same loyalty and discretion.'

Mrs Keppel understood Edward's moods, his pressures, and his depressions. He was good with children and became known to the two young Keppel daughters as 'Kingy'. His most intimate moments with Alice Keppel and her children were at Biarritz where Edward, invariably in good form, would set up picnics. The Keppel children's nanny remembers these excursions with mixed feelings:

' "Kingy" spied out the land for a suitable site and, at his given word, we all stopped and the footmen set out the lunch. Chairs and a table appeared, linen tablecloths, plates, glasses, silver. Every variety of cold food was produced, spiced by iced-cup in silver-plated containers . . . For some unfathomed reason, "Kingy" had a preference for picnicking by the side of the road. On Easter Day inevitably, this was packed with carriages and the first motor-cars, all covered with dust, and when we parked by the roadside, most of the traffic parked with us.'

But the fact that Alice Keppel was friendly with Queen Alexandra does not minimize the Queen's generosity in allowing her helpless husband to see his right-hand mistress. When Edward saw Mrs Keppel he had great difficulty in breathing but was still quite cheerful. He was sitting in an armchair but was later put to bed, where he sank into his final coma. Just before he fell into the coma, Edward muttered, 'No, I shall not give in; I shall go on; I shall work to the last.' It could be argued that these are altogether too altruistic dying words, and that it is more likely that he called for a lobster tea. But in fact it is probable that he did utter these stern words of duty, for Edward believed in his divine right and was likely to go out with such a phrase on his lips. A little after 11.45 pm the Archbishop of Canterbury read a short prayer and the King died. There was considerable grief in the nation that good old Teddy was no more – as well as among the politicians. Asquith recalled his thoughts as he learnt the news while the ship on which he was travelling sailed home through the Bay of Biscay: 'I went up on deck and the first sight that met my eyes in the twilight before dawn was Halley's comet blazing in the sky . . . I felt bewildered and stunned . . . we had lost, without warning or preparation, the Sovereign whose ripe experience,

trained sagacity, equitable judgement and unvarying consideration counted for so much. For two years I had been his Chief
Minister . . . unbroken confidence lightened the load which I
should otherwise have found almost intolerably oppressive.'

The long-suffering Alexandra was heart-broken. She said that
'she had turned into stone, unable to cry, unable to grasp the
meaning of it all, and incapable of doing anything. She would like
to go and hide in the country.' The future King, Prince George,
who was to make a pale, withdrawn and dull monarch in contrast
to his convivial father, wrote in his diary, 'I have lost the best
friend, and the best of fathers. I never had a cross word with him
in my life. I am heart-broken and overwhelmed with grief.'

Rosa Lewis reacted characteristically and flamboyantly to the
news of her former patron's death. Champagne was served at the
Cavendish, the guests raised their glasses to Edward's portrait and
Rosa then led a procession down to a special wine cellar. Here
Rosa stored a battery of vintages that had been reserved exclusively for Edward's table at country house parties. Amongst the
wines were Veuve Clicquot 1904, the Château Pontet-Canet 1895,
and the Schloss Johannisberg Cabinet 1893. There were also
some eighty-year-old brandies, vintage ports and liqueurs. Rosa
locked the door of the cellar and refused to allow it to be opened
again until after her death. It was a fitting epitaph to Edward and
he would have appreciated it.

Rosa was made highly insecure not just by Edward's death but
also by the death of her father, which occurred at almost the same
time. She had kept her family well provided for but she had little
personal connection with them. It must have been brought home
to her, by the sudden death of the two men, just how little she had.
Her father, whom she so despised, at least had loved her in a
roughish way. Excelsior had also loved her in a weakish way.
And it was she who had been the *concierge* paving the way for
Edward's affairs of the heart, she who had had to go through
with an 'arranged' marriage to provide a respectable front. She
must have realized, too, that though she had been involved in the
initiation of so many other people's love affairs, the only people
she had any affection for she often ultimately despised. However,
there was no going back, she recognized that. But after the death
of the King, she must have wondered if there was any point in

going forward. But although she didn't know it then, her need for affection was going to be filled – twofold – by two men who had reached a stage in life at which they also were desperately craving affection.

But first a comment on the ramifications of Edward's death. There is no doubt that no monarch since Edward had been such a public personality. There was a general feeling in the country that he kept things together, and he appeared strong at a time when the imperialistic stability of the nineteenth century was giving way to the imperialistic instability of the twentieth. George lacked personality and was, to say the least, a rather more conventional figure than his father, thus giving Asquith the opportunity to state, 'It is not the function of a constitutional monarch to act as arbiter or mediator between rival parties and policies.' Edward would never have accepted this statement, under any circumstances.

In fact Edward had gained an exaggerated reputation for having an influence on foreign policy. It was his colourful personality that made it *look* as if he did, although it is true to say that his enormous popularity in France played a strong part in bringing about the *entente cordiale* in 1904.

George Dangerfield in *The Strange Death of Liberal England* gives one of the best summaries of Edward's influence and reputation: 'He represented in a concentrated shape, those bourgeois kings whose florid forms and rather dubious escapades were all the industrialized world had left of an ancient divinity; his people saw in him the personification of something nameless, genial and phallic.'

With the ending of the frenetic Edwardian age, reality obtruded all too quickly. The wearisome entertainment was coming to an end and a very new world was emerging. It was not a world that Rosa Lewis was going to appreciate.

Both Sir William Eden and Lord Ribblesdale arrived at the Cavendish at about the same time. Of the two, Eden was distinctly the more boorish. He was also extremely paranoid. For instance, he was quite unable to bear the colour red and would take unparalleled exception to its appearance in anything from a flower garden to a trifle. He had an obsessive aversion to dogs (which makes his residence in the Cavendish appear to be a permanent siege against Rosa's own dogs), couldn't bear anyone whistling and bore a deep hatred for certain styles of architecture such as the front of Buckingham Palace, the Albert Memorial, and Harrods. His relationship with Lady Eden was tempestuous; he hated children and loved prize-fighting, which presumably channelled some of his aggression. He wrote: 'I painted amidst shrieking children, glorying in my annoyance. And people say, why have you such a low opinion of human nature! After all "the child is father of the man". Children are natural and *brutes*!'

Sir William had very few saving graces and it would obviously have been amusing, if not downright dangerous, to stroll into his quarters in the Cavendish whistling, wearing a red waistcoat, with a couple of dogs and some postcards of the front of Buckingham Palace.

Sir William's greatest pleasure was probably his painting, and George Moore wrote of his work, after one of his exhibitions:

> 'Sir William Eden is an amateur: we use the word in its original sense, and can conceive, therefore, no higher epithet of commendation. There are too few amateurs among us. ... A glance at the pictures shows us that he is a painter who travels rather than a traveller who paints. ... How many water-colour artists are there living who need hesitate to sign that tall drawing, some eight inches in height by four in width, representing a narrow jutting street with an awning, under which some turbaned figures are sitting? There is no sky above the street, the picture is without violent relief, a pink and a grey note blended and harmonized and united with refinement and skill. Examine the few lines that appear. Are they not seen with feeling, and are they not feelingly rendered, and is there not the unmistakable beauty of touch of the born artist – of the amateur?'

Sir William had a very abrasive relationship with Rosa but he clung on to the Cavendish as a bolt-hole from his family, as a stage for his self-indulgence, and as a refuge for his idiosyncrasies. His correspondence with Rosa, from his arrival in the annexe next door to the Cavendish in 1911 until his death at the Cavendish in 1915, was classically peppery.

Windlestone
Ferry Hill
30 May 1912

Sir William presents his compliments to Mrs Lewis,
and as he is informed that his rooms are constantly
inspected by visitors – Tom, Dick and Harry – and
that his carpets are getting rapidly worn out, he
must insist for the future on a charge of one guinea
being paid by anyone invading his premises – for
which he must hold Mrs Lewis responsible.

In the same year other admonishing notes appeared, yet each
had an affectionate feel to it – even when they were at their rudest.
For instance: 'Mrs Lewis – Charming woman! Will you *please*
turn out that damned dog before I have to murder it, or *you* – for
choice! Yours, in ever increasing affection, Sir William'
And from Venice he wrote:

Palazzo Ambasciatore
Venice
27 Dec. 1912

Dear Mrs Lewis,
    I hear from someone staying at the Cavendish that
the blankets are filthy! You had better see to this for
your reputation's sake!

Love to all from
Sir William

And in 'friendlier' vein: 'Woman – have you washed the bankets
and swept the crumbs since I left? – Must have a good dinner.
I have had O but filth since I left. I want fried fillets of sole, roast
neck of beautiful sheep. Quails *à la* Mrs Lewis *et voilà* tout.'
    Sir William's prize-fighting activities also came to roost at the
Cavendish.

Windlestone

Dear Mrs Lewis,
    I am coming up crowned in glory on Tuesday.
The Hon. Ashley too. Now look 'ere. I shall have a
dinner-party that night – noblemen, gentlemen,
women, ladies, and prize-fighters – and we will box
in the dining-room after. See? Tell your *Lord*

Ribblesdale I want him, dinner and after, and anyone
else you may think of – pretty – either sex – none
but the brave deserve the fair.

W.E.

This was the beginning of a friendship between the similarly
inclined personalities of Ribblesdale and Eden, which this note
epitomizes:

> Dear Lord Ribblesdale,
>   Lunch with me Cavendish 1.15 on 8th and on my
> private view – there is no need to praise or buy –
> and will you bring that pretty girl, I forget the name,
> *avec les jolies dents* and the right amount of false colour.
> I will try Pamela, and Lady Scarborough is coming, at
> least so she says. I am laid up again with gout that
> damnable virtue which will have its reward.
>
> Ever,   William Eden

After a while Eden persuaded Rosa to have a wall knocked down
between the annexe, 18 Duke Street, and the main body of the
Cavendish. This gave him the best of both worlds – contact with
the raffish set in the hotel, and a private eyrie in which to nurse
his depression and immerse himself in his self-imposed isolation.
Lady Eden occasionally stayed at the hotel, also the children,
Timothy (the late Sir Timothy Eden), Anthony (the late Lord
Avon) and Marjorie, (afterwards Countess of Warwick). But it
seems that Lady Eden preferred to remain at Windlestone, the
family's estate in Durham. At times Eden enjoyed life there too,
but he was soon back at the Cavendish, for to this crusty, selfish,
obsessive old man, the Cavendish was home and Rosa his mother
figure, combatant and drinking companion. She obviously liked
him, although not as much as Ribblesdale. But towards the end
of his life, Eden became even crustier and it was obvious that he
was becoming impossible:

25 May 1914

> Dear Madam,
>   I am sorry to complain and needs must when the devil
> drives, and you are the devil whilst you are amusing
> yourself which is all you do with your lovers, your
> dogs, your cocktails and your caterwauling.

Perhaps because she admired eccentricity in others as well as herself, Rosa put up with Eden admirably. She also liked his independence – linking it perhaps with her own. She told Mary Lawton:

'Sir William always had clever people around him. George Moore came here a lot in those days. I must say I liked him much better than his books. Sir William had Walter Sickert and Shackleton, too, and various sportsmen, clever literary men and artists – all kinds, and he quarrelled with them all in turn, using fierce arguments, fierce and terrifying statements, but they all used to simmer down and remain almost where they commenced, and no man even thought of that as bad temper, because it was always expressed openly to anybody's face. All men and women alike, he served the same, and never did anything behind their backs. Amongst his other accomplishments he was an atheist. I have got a picture upstairs of his idea of Hell. I gave him £10 for it once when he was hard up.'

Apparently not all Eden's energies were channelled into his boxing and he would quite often lose all control in the dining-room, threatening to throw an offending dish in the kitchen-maid's face. Rosa also claimed that this custard-pie slapstick routine was extended to her – 'then he would dirty *my* face with a dish that didn't please him, and he wouldn't even wait – if he was in a furious rage – while I washed for him to do it (knowing that, if he waited for that, he would get over his furious rage) . . . And he was constantly writing me letters – letters of complaint about anything and everything – always very fierce.'

Certainly there is evidence to suggest that he wrote a large number of letters but that he really rubbed Rosa's, or any of her staff's, face in ill-favoured dishes seems a typical Rosa exaggeration

Eden died in his apartments at the Cavendish, petulant to the last. It's difficult to know who mourned him – and to what extent. But his son, Timothy Eden, wrote of his father in *The Tribulations of a Baronet* directly and sympathetically:

'He was a true and loyal friend, a shrewd adviser with a knowledge of the world, a man largely capable of sympathy and love, and sadly needing it; but his uncontrolled rages terrified and drove away an approaching friendship as a bird is scared to a distant branch. His intolerance of the opinions of others not only hurt their natural vanity but made any reasonable discussion impossible. His personal and direct rudeness was offensive to the most patient. His constant and exaggerated irritation with the minor details of life, and the volcanic expression which he gave to his acute suffering from incidental noises, sights and smells – mere nothings which the normal man passes over unnoticed – though amusing at first, became quickly wearisome, if not alarming. It is not easy to understand how a terrible tornado of oaths, screams, gesticulations and flying sticks can be seriously prompted by a barking dog; nor will anyone readily admit that the whistling of a boy in the street can be a good and sufficient reason for breaking a window with a flower-pot. Thus any friendly intercourse with him, though brightened with unique and delightful compensations, could never be reposeful. It was bound to be a guardedly attempted, difficult, dangerous and exciting experiment.'

Lord Ribblesdale, although himself of uncertain temper, was neither a bully nor a boor. Having already lost their son, his wife Charlotte contracted tuberculosis and died in 1911. Ribblesdale was heart-broken and fell into a long, black depression. It had been a good marriage and there was no doubt that he had adored her. They hadn't, however, been entirely faithful to each other throughout their marriage. Ribblesdale had had an affair with Lady Angela, youngest daughter of the Earl of Rosslyn, and Charlotte with Lord Curzon. She was officially forgiven by Ribblesdale and the affair dismissed as a 'clumsy indiscretion'. Quite how Ribblesdale described his affair with Lady Angela is not on record – if he described it at all.

Ribblesdale moved in as a permanent resident at the Cavendish in 1911, eventually selling his London house, moving his own furniture into his suite and giving what was left over to Rosa. There is nothing to suggest that Rosa and Ribblesdale became lovers but there was obviously a very close bond between them – far closer than the one Rosa had with Eden. Ribblesdale had lost his much loved mother in the same year as Charlotte's death and was grief-stricken enough to regard the Cavendish as a sanctuary and Rosa as a mother figure. It would seem that was the role Ribblesdale best liked women to play. Despite his aggressiveness, he was massively sentimental. I've already referred to the 'Dolls' and his very affectionate way with them. Sufficient to say that he referred to Charlotte as his 'Angel Queen', an epithet which carried all too ironic overtones after her death.

Ribblesdale used to accompany Rosa on shopping expeditions. He would also take her out to lunch and occasionally to the theatre. He needed her as a prop and he made Rosa feel very genuinely wanted – for the first time since Excelsior had wanted her so badly. But with Ribblesdale Rosa had somebody she could respect – as well as someone who relied on her. She could also handle him, for although he was not as manic as Eden, he had wild outbursts of temper that still somehow had to be coped with.

Inevitably, this was not to last – the relationship between Ribblesdale and Rosa could only be temporary. Gradually Ribblesdale emerged from his grief. He realized that life still had something to offer. 'To be a lord', he said, 'is still a popular thing . . . to be pleased with yourself may be selfish, or it may be stupid, but it is seldom actively disagreeable.'

Shortly after the lifting of his depression, Ribblesdale remarried, which was obviously a very galling and very serious blow to Rosa. Unfortunately for Ribblesdale's new wife, who was the widow of John Jacob Astor, her maiden name was Willing: Ava Willing. Seizing on this, Rosa made great play with it, using her stage-cockney humour to cover her grief. And as she made very *much* use of it, she must have been very hurt indeed. Quite what she imagined would come out of her relationship with Ribblesdale is difficult to understand – and indeed it is just not possible to say how far the relationship went. But what is clear is that Ribblesdale's presence in the Cavendish was very important indeed, and he left a legacy of bitterness in Rosa Lewis's heart – bitterness against men that was to come out more strongly as the years went by

It was probably the companionship that she had come to rely on most – that, and the fact that he had depended so very much on her. She also liked his idiosyncrasies – and his eccentricities, patronizing though they were. He would buy new clothes for matchsellers, and he dressed two Cavendish kitchen-maids in pure white for their confirmation, giving them two prayer books as souvenirs. He was worried that children ran poverty-stricken in the streets around the hotel and he would say to Rosa, 'Now don't you think all those poor little things must hate to see Diana [his daughter] riding in her carriage?' Rosa claimed she replied swiftly, 'Oh no, my Lord, they say "lovely lady" and they like to see her go.' But even this swift tact was not enough to prevent his grabbing the bewildered children and thrusting them bodily into the carriage.

To Ribblesdale, the Cavendish seemed to represent some kind of extended family, and even in his more formal letters it was obvious how very fond of Rosa he was.

> Easton Grey,
> Malmesbury.
> Christmas Day.

My dear Rosa Lewis,

The children and their mother [Ribblesdale's daughter] are enchanted with the little men's purses and also with the toys. We all agree only Rosa Lewis wd. have thought of and found the little purses. Barbara and Diana are pleased with their blankets – and I hope you have sent one to Laura. I feel sure you have, as it was your determination that she should not be left in the cold when yellow blankets were strong. That is 2 I owe you for as well as the 3 I owe Walpole Bros. for and you must also let me know what the toys for the Masters Wilson cost.

The game pie and the pâté are much appreciated and Mrs Graham Smith is going to write to you herself. Alas – she is very lame and crippled – but in good spirits – very brave and never gives in.

I return on Thursday, and now this post takes you all best Xmas and New Year wishes.

> Vy.
>
> R

Barbara sends you her love and thanks for the toys to her children.

Another aspect of the Cavendish life which Ribblesdale took pleasure in participating in was the annual servants' ball – a function that continued right up until the beginning of the First World War. Rosa also invited (or compelled) some forty other regular clients to come to these balls, which she held for a strange mixture of reasons – partly to patronize, partly to please, and partly to show her staff 'the other side of life'. Everything was the same as for an ordinary ball – the band, the flowers, the floor and the menu. With devastating innacuracy, Rosa told Mary Lawton: '. . . the people who have worked for me are just as well off as the people who work for a millionaire, because no one can live or be with me without getting something, and they must be of some good or no good at all, and if they are no good – out they go! . . . I have no method, no time limit, and I don't believe in your eight hours' day. I think if everybody would work when they do work, or when they were needed, and took their pleasure and their rest when they were not needed, it would average up the eight hours a day with eighteen hours' pay.'

It is not on record whether Rosa paid these rates, although it would seem very doubtful. However, what she *did* try to do was to run the Cavendish in the same feudal way as she had seen some of the great houses run. At her own ball, with Lord Ribblesdale leading off the dancing with her head cook, Rosa Lewis was, for one night of the year, a lady. A society hostess who was graciously entertaining, and seeing in her own servants the joys of aristocratic family life. 'My cook', she said, 'photographed in evening dress looks as good as anybody – as good as a Duchess. The little scullery maid in a nice little evening frock, showing a certain amount of neck, and with her hair nicely dressed, looks charming. The laundress, dressed up as a fine lady, looks as well as the best in the land, I can assure you.' And Rosa herself could be assured that she, too, looked the best in the land on that one special night of fantasy.

Ragtime and public drama were very central features of the years leading up to the First World War. The sinister farce of Dr Crippen's thwarted flight in 1910, the controversial direction of the Sidney Street siege in 1911 by the young Winston Churchill, the massive national shock of the *Titanic* disaster in 1912, and the tragic loss of Captain Scott and his comrades in 1913 moved the nation with a feeling of high drama. Meanwhile it was 'Hullo Ragtime' in London and the changing mood provoked a new atmosphere in the Cavendish. There was an increasing sense of 'clubbishness' about the place, and supper parties suddenly became the rage. The young aristocrats would entertain Gaiety girls, whilst the older Stage-door Johnny types would entertain the popular actresses of the time. Already the 'heaviness' of Edwardian-style gaiety was passing and there was a new, lighter, more sophisticated touch to entertainment and to fashion.

Rosa remained in her period and continued to wear Edwardian-style clothes. Her hair was growing grey and she cut a distinguished if slightly dated figure. Already she was resisting change. However, she was commercially adaptable enough to more than adequately set the scene for the Gaiety girl and Stage-door Johnny supper parties. She did so by choosing the right kind of room with the right kind of décor, soft lights, and so on, without changing the Edwardian atmosphere. All the trappings of room-service seduction.

Hullo Ragtime ran for 451 performances at the London Hippodrome (now The Talk of the Town) and was a fairly amazing piece of work. Even Rupert Brooke saw it ten times and dragged all his friends to see it. Ethel Levey belted out the big numbers whilst Shirley Kellogg, looking like an overdressed drum-majorette, led her ragtime chorus along the joy plank at right angles to the stage, giving the audience an eyeful of long boots, stocking-encased knees and skirts draped just above them. Nevertheless it was all considered very naughty and the show was the precursor to songs such as 'Hitchy Koo' and 'Alexander's Ragtime Band', and dances such as the Turkey Trot and the Bunny Hug. It was a great shame that the gregarious Edward had not lived long enought to participate in this period. He would have Turkey Trotted with the best of them and he might even have braved the Cavendish to allow the royal roving eye to fall on a well-fleshed Gaiety girl at one of Mrs Lewis's little supper parties. It would have been impossible to imagine the current royal incumbent, George, letting his hair down or being in any way disreputable – which was good for the constitution and bad for charisma.

Hullo Ragtime was replaced at the same theatre by *Hullo Tango* which was considered even more lascivious. As J.B.Priestley wrote in his book, *The Edwardians*:

'It was denounced along a wide front as an immodest dance of low South American origin, a kind of going-to-the-dogs in a very elaborate fashion. What next? – when hotels were offering tango teas and ladies who ought to have known better were actually giving tango parties. The men, not all of them young, were trying to look like the riffraff of Rio. Girls of decent parentage and upbringing were swaying and slinking into perdition. There were thunders from pulpits, letters quivering with indignation in the press. What was the country coming to?'

With all the current crazes and money still plentiful, the Cavendish was doing very well indeed financially. The Empire prospered, motor cars were maturing, the trains seemed to be all crack expresses and the aeroplane was in its infancy. Ribblesdale still leant on Rosa and Eden still berated her. She was happy amidst bounding eccentricity. A typical example of this was the way the Cavendish porter, Scott, addressed most of his internal notes to Rosa to her pet dog – signed by his own pet dog. When his dog, called Freddy, died, Scott had him stuffed and presented the inanimate object to a surprised and horrified Lord Ribblesdale. And however Ribblesdale tried to get rid of Freddy, the more Scott returned him to his ungrateful new owner.

Scott, like many of the Cavendish servants, was odd. According to Rosa, he had few vices bar occasional gambling and an aversion to water. This also included bath water, but for some mysterious, nay miraculous, reason he never smelt. Apart from Lord Ribblesdale's macabre present, he used Freddy for various other strange tasks, although only during his lifetime. Usually Scott went to meet Cavendish clients at the various stations in London and in celebration of a safe end to a journey he would tie ribbons on his pet. So if you happened to be the fifteenth guest arriving at the station that day you would be greeted by Freddy and his unwashed master, the dog being hung with fifteen ribbons. Should the guests be Scottish, then Freddy would wear tartan ribbons, and should they be interested in racing, then Freddy would proudly bear their colours. This almost surreal situation extended to clients' marriages, when Freddy would be taken to Westminster Abbey, and to Freddy's own sex life – bitches would be procured for him by Scott at a shilling a go.

When Lord Ribblesdale forgot the anniversary of his wife's death, Freddy appeared clad in black crape, which could only have further depressed the neurotic Peer – although the final *coup de grâce*, the presentation of the stuffed, dead dog, must have made Ribblesdale strongly question the length of his stay at the Cavendish – despite Rosa's home comforts.

The catering service continued to flourish and Rosa organized all the Foreign Office dinners from 1909 until 1911, as well as renting and equipping large town houses for one-night parties. Lord Ribblesdale's daughter was married from Surrey House at 27 Grosvenor Square in great style, with Rosa at her most lavish. She would hire furniture (or use some from the Cavendish) and generally refurbish the place. She told Mary Lawton, with amazing blandness, that she had practically rebuilt the houses. 'I would take an empty house, and furnish it just for the night, in competition against all other catering people. I'd furnish up a place, put in windows, take out windows, build up staircases, put lights inside and out, in about twelve hours.'

The lightning builder! On this basis she deserved to lend her considerable talents to industries outside catering. On a more realistic note, she continued, 'It would cost about £700 to £800, including supper, wine, waiters, and flowers, unless you were very extravagant.' (It was Mrs Lewis who was extravagant.) 'I didn't believe in spending more than £30 on flowers.' Rosa produced a wedding breakfast for a Gaiety girl who married into the aristocracy (Mrs Sterling, who was united with Lord Rocksavage's brother). Also during this period she cooked for the Chancellor of the Exchequer, the Duchess of Sutherland, Asquith, Lloyd-George, Balfour, Sargent and Roosevelt. These were amongst the more celebrated on a very starry list and Rosa still spent most week-ends at Hever Castle, satisfying Waldorf Astor's appetite.

Alfred Harmsworth was another distinguished guest at the Cavendish and it was here that he spent much of his time. Later to become Lord Northcliffe, Alfred Harmsworth had been born into a middle-class Victorian family and had made a considerable fortune out of popular periodicals such as *Answers* and *Comic Cuts* before he was thirty. Throughout the South African War, and during the years leading up to the First World War, Harmsworth pioneered a brand of journalism that was a complete break-through in mass communication – indeed, until Reith, his was the greatest influence ever upon public communication. By 1895 Harmsworth's home-spun collection included *Home Sweet Home*, *The Halfpenny Marvel*, *Home Chat* and *Union Jack* amongst other magazines. He also owned the *Evening News*, and on 4 May 1896 he launched the *Daily Mail*. Commenting on the current state of the press, Harmsworth wrote in his autobiography:

> '*The Times* went its own mysterious way in the warren of Printing House Square. The *Daily Telegraph* continued its gentle rivalry with the *Standard*, the *Morning Post* was alive, the *Daily News*, political and literary, was the leading radical organ, and the *Daily Chronicle*, under Massingham, was the most brilliant and enterprising of all. I hope I shall not offend my friends of those great dailies when I say that their lack of initiative, through which they had fallen from the highly competitive days of the sixties, and their subservience to Party, were a direct invitation to the assault administered by the *Daily Mail*.'

By the time Northcliffe (as he was by then) cast a predatory eye on *The Times*, he already owned the *Observer* with the great J.L. Garvin to edit it, although it was not until Northcliffe parted company with that newspaper that Garvin really came into his own. On 16 March 1908, Northcliffe became chief proprietor of *The Times* at the cost of £320,000. Edward VII was not amused and pointed out that if Northcliffe ran into trouble with the paper, something should be done to prevent it from coming under worse ownership. He commented, 'There are so many fools who like titles that it ought not to be difficult to raise money.'

Harmsworth liked the curious atmosphere of the Cavendish, its aristocratic overtones and Rosa's personality. The liking was reciprocated, and Rosa told Mary Lawton: 'He had a rare indi-vidual charm. I have some nice letters from him to me. He used always to send me a lovely simple kind of scent and soaps from Cannes. He never forgot it. He was very thoughtful and very

courteous.' He was also very adroit, for his presence in the Cavendish attracted both politicians and generals alike. They may have
despised his cheap newspapers – but they were also extremely
frightened of them.

Harmsworth saw copy in Rosa and she was not loath to
cooperate; she identified with Harmsworth's newspapers and she
admired their chirpy, brash style. Harmsworth called Jimmy
Heddle, Editor of the *Daily Sketch*, and asked him to do the
necessary. Heddle did it in some style, taking the entire front
page of the *Sketch* for the purpose on 13 June 1914. The banner
headline read: 'ENGLISHWOMEN CAN BE THE BEST COOKS IN
THE WORLD, SAYS MRS. ROSA LEWIS, MOST FAMOUS OF
WOMEN CHEFS, ONCE A KITCHEN MAID'.

Underneath the headline came four large photographs. The
first showed Rosa in full evening dress, the second showed her in
the Cavendish kitchen, the third showed Rosa and the girls hard
at work (the caption read: 'Keep your kitchen bright, encourage
your assistants, and they will take an interest in work'), and the
fourth showed an idyllic, near convent-like scene with Rosa and
her girls, dressed in full catering service regalia, standing in the
centre quadrangle of the Cavendish, surrounded by flowers.
Underneath the pictures the text read:

'Why shouldn't Englishwomen be the best cooks in the
world? The most famous woman chef in the world is an Englishwoman, Mrs Rosa Lewis, and she says they can be. Mrs Lewis
began in the kitchen as a scullery maid. Now in her own
West-End hotel she cooks for Kings, Emperors, Princes and
Ambassadors. At Coronation time some of the highest people
in the world enjoyed her wonderful dishes. And she never had
a cooking lesson in her life. "Encourage the Englishwoman,"
says Mrs Lewis, "pay her good wages, take an interest in her
work, and she will be the best cook of all." '

A classic Rosa over-simplification but unmistakably the kind of
interview she would give. A few days later, on 18 June 1914, the
same newspaper ran a nationwide cookery competition, with
Rosa Lewis presiding over it as judge. The headline ran:

£10 FOR SIX DINNER MENUS

Scheme to Encourage Women to Learn Cooking

HAVE YOU SENT IN YOUR LIST?

World's Most Famous Woman Cook to Judge Competition.

'The article on the career of Mrs Rosa Lewis, the most famous woman cook in the world, published recently in the *Daily Sketch*, has aroused tremendous interest among housewives, chefs and girls, and Mrs Lewis has received a large number of applications from young women anxious to learn cooking by entering her service as kitchen or scullery maid.

With a view to encouraging these girls, the *Daily Sketch*, as previously announced, is offering a prize of £10 for the best six dinner menus sent in for a week in June, the condition being that competitors must not exceed a sum of £3 for the week's cooking.'

There was certainly a supreme irony in the last line, considering how much Rosa boasted that she charged for her catering service, and indeed how much she charged in actuality. Rosa's press fame, however, was not to last, as world events quickly intervened.

The Archduke Franz Ferdinand was assassinated on 28 June 1914, and Britain declared war on Germany on 4 August 1914. As an un-nostalgic assessment of the Edwardian era and after, no prose is as objective as A. J. P. Taylor's writing in his *From Sarajevo to Potsdam*:

'In 1914 Europe was a single civilized community, more so than even at the height of the Roman Empire. A man could travel across the length and breadth of the Continent without a passport until he reached the frontiers of Russia and the Ottoman Empire. He could settle in a foreign country for work or pleasure without legal formalities, except, occasionally, some health requirements. Every currency was as good as gold, although this security rested ultimately on the skills of financiers in the City of London. There were common political forms. Though there were only two republics in Europe (France and Portugal – Switzerland was technically a confederation, not a republic), every state except Monaco possessed some form of constitution limiting the power of the monarch to a greater or lesser degree. Nearly everywhere men could be sure of reasonably fair treatment in the courts of law. No one was killed for religious reasons. No one was killed for political reasons, despite the somewhat synthetic bitterness often shown in political disputes. Private property was everywhere secure, and in nearly all countries something was done to temper the extreme rigours of poverty.'

The first action that Rosa took on the declaration of war, was to take down the signed photograph of her much-admired Kaiser – and hang it in the lavatory. But she was not to realize how many of her most favoured clients were to lose children on the great muddy European plains of war. Neither was she to realize that the so-called golden age of Edwardian England was over. With its passing Rosa Lewis lost the world she had loved – and to which she belonged. She was now to be a woman out of her time.

FIVE

War—and its Aftermath
1914–26

'... Since 1914, now that they are all gone, I do not consider
anything that I do of any value.'
ROSA LEWIS

THROUGHOUT THE ENTIRE PERIOD OF THE FIRST WORLD WAR, the Cavendish became a social first-aid post both to those who could afford it – and to those who couldn't. The Royal Flying Corps and the Americans were amongst Rosa's favourites but basically anyone in uniform was more than welcome. However, any man out of uniform, unless old, senile, infirm or sick, would *not* get such a warm response. But to those returning from the horrors of the trenches or aerial combat, Rosa could provide certain necessary, mind-obliterating services. Like alcohol and whores – 'Nice clean ones', as she would have said.

She was, of course, appalled by the loss of life. The second generation, the sons of the first Cavendish set, had already passed through their initiation into the hotel. Now they were dying like flies. Perhaps one of the best illustrations of the type of hell in which they died is given by Siegfried Sassoon in his *Memoirs of an Infantry Officer*. In this sequence he is describing the horrors of a battlefield near the Hindenburg Line to a young officer, fresh from Oxford:

'The wind had dropped and the sunset sky was mountainous with calm clouds. We inspected a tank which had got stuck in the mud while crossing a wide trench. We succeeded in finding this ungainly monster interesting. Higher up the hill the open ground was dotted with British dead. It was an unexpectedly tidy scene, since most of them had been killed by machine-gun fire. Stretcher-bearers had been identifying the bodies and had arranged them in happy warrior attitudes, hands crossed and heads pillowed on haversacks. Often the contents of a man's haversack were scattered around him. There were letters lying about; the pathos of these last letters from home was obvious enough.'

Later he writes of the torture undergone by a party, commanded by him, carrying boxes of trench mortar bombs:

'We were out nearly seven hours; it rained all day and the trenches were a morass of glue-like mud. . . . It was a yellow corpse-like day, more like November than April, and the landscape was desolate and treeless. . . . I can remember a pair of hands (nationality unknown) which protruded from the soaked ashen soil like the roots of a tree turned upside down; one hand seemed to be pointing at the sky with an accusing gesture. Each time I passed that place the protest of those fingers became more expressive of an appeal to God in defiance of those who made the war. Who made the war? I laughed hysterically as the thought passed through my mud-stained mind.'

Sassoon's demonic description more than emphasizes the need for the blotting out of those scenes from the minds of the young soldiers – particularly when they had to face it all again when their leave was over. And where better to blot it out than in the alcohol-bemused suites of the Cavendish? The fading romanticism of the Elinor Glyn room repeatedly saw drunken parties of young men who only wanted to forget, not just the ugly, violent, recent past, but the ugly, violent, near future to which they would shortly have to return.

The death roll also affected the two most permanent residents of the Cavendish, Ribblesdale and Eden, but in two very different ways. Ribblesdale's was a double tragedy – his son-in-law who had married his daughter only a few months previously and for whom Rosa had given such a lavish reception, was killed in action. Then, later, his son Charles died of his wounds on board a hospital ship. Despite his later marriage, Ribblesdale never recovered from these losses.

In 1915 Sir William Eden died peacefully in his suite at the Cavendish. Somewhat idealistically, Rosa told Mary Lawton, 'Sir William sent me the last letter he ever wrote. He was dying for a week, and I was with him when he actually died. It was the most beautiful deathbed I have ever seen. He died exactly as he lived, and died as I would like to die. Everything around him had to be beautiful and fair – clean and exacting to the end.' Frankly, the thought of Sir William's dying 'exactly as he lived' summons up an alarming choleric picture, but perhaps the crusty baronet was less abrasive in death.

As one survivor of trench warfare put it, 'You've never seen rats till you've seen rats that were born, and fed, and grew in human flesh.' Rosa knew all too well that these were the sights her boys had to face when they left her. She must also have seen, all too clearly, the results of shock and fear on the young men who came to her. This lance-corporal, for instance, is a typical case and the discovery of him is narrated by a Sapper: 'We went outside and found him huddled up in an empty dugout. "Come out," Jock called to him. He didn't move, but glared at us like a scared animal, his teeth chattering and hands clinched together, letting out a low moan more like a growl at intervals.'

Every time a man emerged from the fantasy world of the Cavendish and prepared to make the grim journey to the front again, Rosa would load him with food parcels, cigarettes, cigars, wine, champagne and various goodies black-marketed from Fortnum's and other emporia. There was no doubt about the fact that she regarded these young men as her own 'boys' and her surrogate mothership was absolutely genuine. She grieved deeply over the ones who didn't come back – and rejoiced in the few who did. There are thousands of testimonies to Rosa's generosities in the First World War, but just two will be sufficient to illustrate what a haven the Cavendish was – and how Rosa was ever loathe to charge for some of her 'boys' mind-blotting.

One of Sir William Eden's sons, Anthony, the late Lord Avon, was a young army officer. He remembered, 'as a very young officer of the First World War, how much kindness Mrs Lewis showed me when on leave. One could always be sure of a glass of champagne if one called on her at any time, and the charge never appeared on my bill.'

Major R. Chandos Bryant, who was in the Queen's Royal Regiment and the Royal Flying Corps, remembered, 'My first visit was as a young subaltern in the early days of the Kaiser's war. I was spending a few days' leave there. Each evening a full bottle of champagne, brandy and whisky was left in my room. As funds were running a bit short, I confined myself to a daily bottle of the fizz. It was a mistake; I should have drunk the lot,

On asking for my bill, on leaving, I was old that Mrs Lewis was very fond of RFC pilots, that I was a guest of the Cavendish, and there was no charge for my stay or drinks.'

In fact the charge probably went on the bill of somebody else who was rich enough to stand it and who for some reason was out of favour with Rosa. But she did not confine her hospitality merely to those who appeared on her doorstep. She often drove to Victoria Station, there to pick up and bring back to the Cavendish men on leave who had nowhere to go. Once in her hotel they entered what must have seemed to them to be a free, alcoholic, orgiastic dream world. All Rosa's frustrated maternal instincts were out in full flower as she cosseted her boys before they died in the mud – or survived to be eternally grateful to her. As they lay shivering in rat-infested trenches they must have looked back wonderingly at the garish freedom of the Cavendish. Perhaps they also looked back wonderingly as they died.

Carroll Carstairs, a young American who joined the Grenadier Guards, wrote a novel called *A Generation Missing*. He was the first author to fictionalize Rosa and the Cavendish, and there was no doubt she was pleased with his personification of her. Far more pleased, anyway, than she was years later when she appeared as Lottie Crump in Evelyn Waugh's *Vile Bodies*. Carstairs wrote:

> 'Something of the excitement, the heightened spirits and energy generated by the War seemed to me to be concentrated in the small space by the four walls of Mrs Oliver's sitting room. Through the clouds of cigarette smoke I could see myself in battle; a drink too much and I felt a reckless courage in the face of an imagined danger. During these lapses a word or a laugh near me, whose immediate significance was not quite understood, seemed like the encouragement and applause of my brother officers. I would leave the Bentinckt with quite a swagger although I was not even in the Army at the time.'

During the First World War, for obvious reasons, the Cavendish lost a good deal of money. Also Rosa had very little help in running the hotel. A niece and an old woman were her only helpmates and it seems that most meals were communally prepared by Rosa, her staff and guests. But her 'boys' were not the only guests of the Cavendish during the First World War. The politicians, particularly Lloyd George, still came. The generals, Kitchener, Roberts, and Cowans, discussed policy there. And the less specifically celebrated came to drink and to socialize. Amongst these were Ellen Terry, Mrs Patrick Campbell and her gruesome lapdog Pinky Panky Poo which had cataracts on both eyes, was practically hairless and had an aggressive tendency, Yvonne Arnaud, Isadora Duncan, J.M.Barrie and Pauline Chase. A mixed bag of talent who no doubt paid through the nose for the comforts of Rosa's 'boys' – as well they should have done!

During this period a profile of Rosa appeared in the *New Yorker* – a profile of which she particularly disapproved. In fact she approved of very little of what was written about her, and even the interviews with Mary Lawton were condemned when they were published in America under the admittedly grisly title *Queen of Cooks – And Some Kings*, by Boni and Liveright in 1926. They were not published in England. The reason Rosa hated them must surely lie in the fact that, under interview, she even further exaggerated her cockney sparrow act, as can be seen from the extracts used in the text of this book. As a result she saw openly published such a tissue of lies that a growing shame – and guilt – made her reject them.

A strange and haunting comfort was given to Lord Ribblesdale, after the death of his son, by Viola and Iris Tree, Sir Herbert Beerbohm Tree's daughters, and Rosa herself. He had already admired Viola's Ariel in Beerbohm Tree's production of *The Tempest* and Iris shared his passion for painting. The rather mystic Tree girls invited Ribblesdale and Rosa down to their house at Robertsbridge in Sussex during the war years, and there the four of them enjoyed short bursts of a rustic idyll. They dressed up, had picnics in the fields, fended for themselves domestically, and escaped from the war; Rosa from the misery of the fate of her boys – and Ribblesdale from the misery of his bereavement. Rosa fondly remembered that 'Going to Robertsbridge really pleased him. Sitting in a field with a huge cup of tea and a bun and butter that he was fond of (a certain bun he would always have from a certain shop) – it was just the sympathy and understanding that made him happy.' Iris drew a sketch of the mourning Ribblesdale and Rosa took it back to the Cavendish, framed it and hung it in her parlour.

Despite the war, Rosa continued to cook, although she mainly catered for the emotional farewell dinners held in the Elinor Glyn room. They were attended by Lloyd George, Asquith, Winston Churchill, Lord French, Kitchener and General Byng amongst other celebrities. She also cooked for Foreign Office functions and this letter certainly proves how highly she was still regarded:

FOREIGN OFFICE
26 July 1917

Dear Mrs Lewis,

Pending the settlement of your account. I can only say on behalf of all who took part, that it never *can* be squared – except as far as the mere financial side is concerned. We should all be bankrupt of language long before we had at all adequately expressed our gratitude and delight in Tuesday's masterpiece; such a feast is cheaply bought at the price of lifelong matrimony (for someone else); and for such another, at your hands, one might even contemplate matrimony on one's own account!

Yr. Sly,
Reginald Farrer

As the war dragged on Rosa was delighted to have ninety soldiers billeted in one part of the Cavendish. The hotel's garage was turned into a canteen for Belgian soldiers and the foyer and corridors were festooned with the crutches of the wounded. Perhaps the greatest and most personal blow came when General Rawlinson gently broke the news to her that two of the boys for whom she had cooked christening dinners, David Bingham and Percy Wyndham, had been killed.

Every morning when a man left the Cavendish for France, Rosa would call him herself, give him his package of goodies and then see him off. Not much of what Rosa told Mary Lawton is personally revealing but she was utterly sincere when she bitterly said:

'Since 1914, now that they are all gone, I do not consider anything that I do of any value ... At the moment War broke out I was at the height of my glory – very successful and a great deal better off than I thought I was, never dreaming that the War would last more than four months – never changing this idea until Armistice day – always saying to myself "It will be over tomorrow." Entirely worked to death, and my brain almost turned, with no thought for anything but the people who were going and coming, and losing their lives. Life became the War and the War only. Always thinking that when it ended I should be where I was in 1914, with the same world, the same people, the same everything. But every year it got worse. The War is the only thing that ever brought real grief and real despair into my life. It used to take me months to get over each person I knew who died. I forced every man I came in contact with to join, and I had a white feather for every man in the back yard and everywhere around, who didn't join. Therefore I was left with hardly a man to carry the coals. I had only old Scott, and sometimes one other.

All the boys I had known, and their mothers and fathers before them, were all allowed to give dinners here, and go down into the cellar and into the kitchen, and help themselves, because everybody's home being shut up, and most people being as crazy as myself, with no homes for their children, I made a home for all here. With money, without money, with crutches and without crutches, with legs, and without legs. I made all the pleasure I could for them, but none were allowed in my house that hadn't been in the War.'

As the First World War drew to its desolate and bloody conclusion, the Cavendish looked as if it had been through a war itself. The rooms had a burnt-out feeling as if all the desperate, hectic gaiety had stripped the walls of paint and the furniture of sheen. It had certainly stripped the place of booze, and despite what must have been a good bit of black-marketeering, Rosa was once again facing bankruptcy.

Did Rosa think her 'boys' were grateful enough to her for all she did for them? Perhaps she didn't. Perhaps she didn't realize *all* she had done for them. For this was Rosa at her genuine best – and she was to repeat the performance in the Second World War too. But the carnage in that war, and the primitiveness of it, was not as great as in the First. It is hard to imagine those torn and bloodied landscapes, those barren fields of broken men and machinery. It is even harder to imagine how eighteen-year-old boys faced the reality of death. But it is not so difficult to imagine how some of them, those *habitués* of the Cavendish, were able to face the return to that reality. For Rosa had provided them with a bolt-hole that healed. A warm cavern of delights that temporarily sheltered them from the corpses and shells and fear and pain of those sodden horizons.

By 1918 Rosa was fifty-one. The Armistice was celebrated as frantically at the Cavendish as anywhere else in London. With one million British dead, the survivors really saw themselves as survivors. Newsboys ran through the streets with the good tidings and the street parties were classless and euphoric. A housewife war-diarist wrote on 11 November 1918:

> 'I was trying to write a coherent letter this morning when all of a sudden the air was rent by a tremendous Bang!! My instant thought was – a raid! – – – But when another great explosion shook the windows and the hooters at Woolwich began to scream like things demented, and the guns started frantically firing all round us like an almighty fugue (!) I knew that this was no raid, but the signing of the armistice had been accomplished! Signal upon signal took up the news; the glorious pulverizing news – that the end had come at last.'

Everyone believed they were now about to move into a new Golden Age, a land fit for heroes. The war had been so much hell – surely a reward was due at its conclusion. That this reward might never come did not occur to anyone.

The King was fifty-three – an erect, dignified and highly respectable figure – as was his Queen. Their court was sober and unpromiscuous, a great contrast to Edward's. The only semi-reprobate was the Prince of Wales, who had inherited some, if not all, of Edward's love of good-timing. This worried George considerably but there was little he could do about it. Despite this, the monarchy was at its strongest, particularly in contrast to the disrupted state of the monarchy elsewhere, with the defeat of Germany and Austria, the unrest in Greece and the Balkans and revolution in Russia. Suddenly there seemed to be more royalty in exile than on thrones and yet, in Britain, the monarchy had been restored to the same rock-like stability that Victoria had enjoyed.

Shortly after the Armistice the President of the United States, Woodrow Wilson, and his wife arrived for celebratory pomp and circumstance. Buckingham Palace was redecorated for the occasion and an Edwardian-style banquet was served in the white and gold ballroom. Gold candelabra, neo-classical mouldings and door frames, and the canopy of crimson velvet lined with Indian silk above the throne – all served to give an impression of great splendour. The only element missing in this massive state binge was personality and although George was dignified and diplomatic, the very essence of Edward's showman royalty was sadly missing.

The debutante system was reintroduced and clothes, despite economies, were more than lavish. One such candidate for royal favour wore 'silver lace over turquoise georgette with side panels of brocaded georgette caught with jewelled ornaments, completed with a brocaded train hung from the shoulders of the corsage'. Presentation was an expensive business, for a house had to be rented at a 'good address' and hand-printed invitation cards, embossed notepaper and vast entertaining bills were also essential factors. But, like the missing Edward at the state banquet, the new debutante system also had its vital missing person – Rosa Lewis. For Rosa had decided to abandon her catering service and concentrate on the Cavendish. The chief reason probably lay in her still-continuing grief for her dead 'boys' and the fact that to cater again for young, stylish people – with so many young, stylish people dead – seemed positively indecent. There were subsidiary reasons, too. She felt as 'burnt out' as the Cavendish after the war, and her former massive energy was beginning to desert her. Her court was now firmly established at the hotel and those who wished to join would come to her. No longer would she go to them. Many debs of course did go to her, largely because Mummy thought the Cavendish had a rather risqué reputation and forbade them entry. This, of course, made them go.

The Prince of Wales headed the smart set of the time but it was not a decadent smart set as Edward's had been. It was fun-loving, travel-hungry, informal and vacuous. It was also harmless and the Prince of Wales, who was young, good-looking and modest, became a very popular figure. His sense of duty was as sound as his father's and grandfather's, and so it was only his parents' restrained personalities and social inhibitions that made them worry about his public image. How fatuous the worries were is well illustrated by their attitude to a photograph which appeared in an American paper, of the Prince and his companion Mountbatten in a swimming pool. All that could be seen were their heads, but it was enough for the conservative George to write stating that it was 'not decent – you might as well be naked'.

It would have helped the Prince to have had his grandfather's stamina but it is easy to appreciate and understand his problems. Particularly when his father irritably wrote, 'I see David continues to dance every night and most of the night. People who don't know will begin to think that either he is mad or the biggest rake in Europe. Such a pity.' In fact it was more of a pity that the reactionary George didn't understand his son's problems better. But royal tradition dies hard.

The Prince of Wales's sense of duty should be emphasized and he wrote about the exhaustion of his tours in his own book, *A King's Story*:

'Whenever I entered a crowd it closed round me like an octopus ... Midnight often found me with wearied brain and dragging feet and the orchestra blaring out the by-now hackneyed tunes. If, mindful of next morning's programme, I were to suggest leaving a party early in order to make up some sleep, or if in an unguarded moment my expression betrayed the utter fatigue that possessed me, my hosts, who no doubt had spent weeks preparing an elaborate and expensive party in my honour, would disappointedly attribute my attitude to boredom, or, what was worse, bad manners. And so I drove myself many a night to the edge of exhaustion, lest unfounded rumour create the suspicion that I was an *Ungracious Prince*.'

In London the Prince's social whirl revolved around the Embassy Club in Old Bond Street where Ambrose was the resident band-leader. The leader of fashion in his set was the Hon. Mrs Dudley Ward, who startled everyone by appearing in the Embassy one night clad in a backless evening dress, a long scarf, artificial flowers on her shoulder and her bare arms decorated with wrist chains and bracelets. *Soigné* is the only untranslatable word that could possibly sum up Mrs Ward's appearance – and the appearance of thousands of other rich young women as they hurried to copy her. Mascara, rouge and lipstick were now used prodigiously for the first time and cosmetic advertising became more militant. But it was not just in fashion that the Prince of Wales's set led society – it was in life-style. Though for them the life-style was very public, very frantic, very innocent. There was certainly no question of royal assignations, discreet apartments run by Mrs Lewis, divorce scandals, card scandals, illegal gaming, hard drinking and mistresses. Tinsel gaiety was the mood and lots of frivolous laughter. Besides the redoubtable Mrs Ward other leading members of the Prince's set included 'Dickie' Mountbatten, 'Fruity' Metcalfe, ex-Indian Cavalry, Paula Gellibrand who distinguished herself by turning up at the Ritz in a hat covered with wistaria, Lady Brownlow and her sister the Hon. Mrs Richard Norton, Rosa's idol Poppy Baring and of course one of the most famous of the set, Lady Diana Cooper, the youngest daughter of the Duke of Rutland, and a *habituée* of the Cavendish. She had been part of the Cavendish set before the war, when as Diana Manners she was mixing with the young Tennants, Asquiths, Grenfells, Listers, Charterises and Herberts. Many of the sons were now dead and Stella Margetson, in her book, *The Long Party*, refers to the wartime parties 'at the Cavendish, with Mrs Lewis leading her Comus crew around and around and into a room where a man was dying (not *in extremis*) "to take his mind off" or to fetch from the cellar Lord Somebody's champagne'.

Diana Manners married Duff Cooper in 1919 when he was a clerk in the Foreign Office. From her house in Gower Street she ran massive parties packed with famous names. But it was not her parties that made her famous; it was her 'style'. Style was something that Lady Diana developed as consciously and as conscientiously as Rosa had developed her own 'stage' personality. As the living statue of the Madonna in the play *The Miracle*, she was highly successful in both New York and London. She was, of course, one of the great beauties of the age and knew it. But it was style that she chiefly cultivated – and it was indeed this that typified the post-war years. *Outré*, 'modern', *soigné*, 'the thing' – all were trend-setting styles of the smart set and because of this obsession with modishness they 'discovered' the raffish atmosphere of the Cavendish and the now sometimes daunting personality of Rosa. As a result of this 'discovery' the tired old Cavendish suddenly swung into a new lease of life. Because it was suddenly 'the thing'.

In the absence of Ribblesdale and Eden, Rosa was desperately lonely. So, when Edith Jeffrey came to the Cavendish – and stayed – she was overjoyed. Edith Jeffrey and her sister Maud had run a dressmaking business during the war and it was Maud who saw an advertisement Rosa had put in the newspaper. She needed somebody to renovate the war-battered fabrics of the Cavendish and eventually Edith applied for the job and immediately secured it.

Edith was the total opposite to Rosa and this is why the partnership – and close friendship – succeeded so well. She was an efficient book-keeper, she had a retiring personality – and she could 'manage' Rosa. Rosa looked on her as someone to lean on in terms of background administration and more importantly, someone who knew and understood her. Soon, Rosa came to look on Edith and Maud as her 'family' – quite different from her own rejected family and much more warmly regarded. With Edith in the background, Rosa could now hold court with an easy mind and she spent regal hours drinking champagne and dominating people in her parlour throne-room.

With Edith's help, it was not long before Rosa had built up the fortunes of the Cavendish again. But inevitably, she still had considerable surplus energy left over, and without the catering service, this needed using. Rosa channelled it into a series of different purchases, beginning with bits and pieces of Dorchester House. After the war it was no longer financially practicable to run the great aristocratic entertainment palaces and one such victim was Dorchester House. At the sale of its contents, Rosa bought eight hundred and fifty pounds' worth of murals, as well as a number of pictures and mirrors. But this was the more conventional side of her purchases for she also bought, for reasons ranging from sentimentality to idiosyncrasy, cast-iron balustrades, tons of stone coping, carved mantlepieces, parquet flooring and a marble staircase which had originally cost £25,000 and was knocked down to Rosa at less than £100.

William Ovenden, Rosa's father, had a small undertaking/watchmaking business in Leyton.

The first step in Rosa's spectacular career: employment with the Comte and Comtesse de Paris

Private apartments for private activities: 55 Eaton Terrace

Rosa: Guevara's idealistic portrait, exhibited at the Royal Academy in the mid-twenties

Ribblesdale, the grim
Ancestor

An early exterior of the Cavendish with its
own private bus. Sir William Eden looks on
menacingly.

Early days at the Cavendish. Rosa is standing
on the right.

Rosa's fleet of cooks

Scott, the porter, and his
infamous dog, Freddy, with
Rosa and the puppies

The Cavendish of the early thirties

One of Rosa's more exotic menus

Menu

Crème de Santé aux Herbes

Barbue à la Meunière

Médaillons de Gibier Épicure

Hanche de Venaison
Selle de Mouton

Grouses Rôties
Salade Cardinal

Choux-fleurs Maître d'hôtel

Poires Darembert
Papillons

Friandises Gorgone

The famous
entrance hall

The dining room

The court yard

Rosa supervising the running of the Cavendish

The ever-loving
Kippy: there were
many Kippies!

The Cavendish of the forties: the kitchens

Rosa's memento-strewn parlour

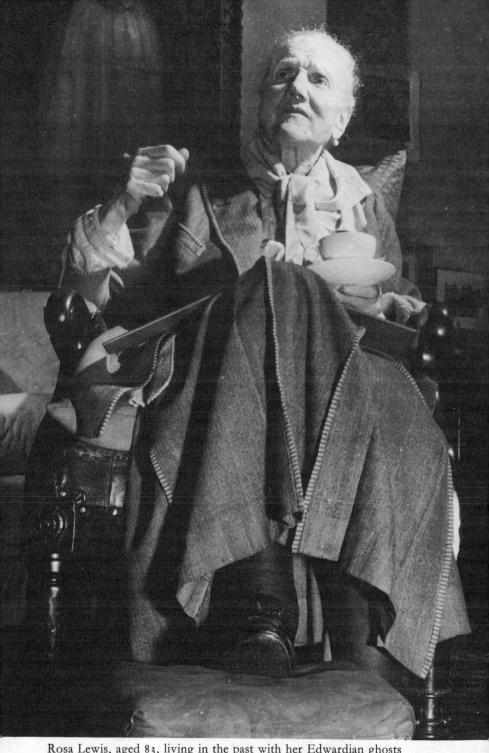

Rosa Lewis, aged 83, living in the past with her Edwardian ghosts

Many of these larger objects ended their lives in the quadrangle garden of the Cavendish where they quietly rotted or weathered away. But it was not as if she were being merely acquisitive – she was subconsciously trying to save Edward's world, brick by brick. Rosa was a thorough-going Edwardian and was determined not to adjust to the new era. For years after Edward died, much of the Edwardian fabric remained, but now it was being torn down. And Rosa was sadly and instinctively trying to save it, piece by piece.

Rosa's second major acquisition was rather more substantial – and was at least an entirety. In fact it is not clear whether she bought it herself or whether it was bought for her by a military admirer. Either way, the house at Jevington near Eastbourne in Sussex was acquired and was occasionally used as a country extension of the Cavendish by the more residential clientele. As these happened to be mainly eccentrics, alcoholics or the sick, their visits to Jevington were regarded with mixed feelings. Life was little different in the country, as they quickly found out, and soon days at 'The Homestead' became almost identical with days at the Cavendish. But the visits of the decadent lame ducks were very occasional, and Rosa mainly used the place to entertain her close personal friends.

The third acquisition, late in the twenties, was more controversial. For, in the spring of 1925, Rosa put in an anonymous bid for a property at Cowes known as Castle Rock which consisted of a small house and garden with a separate pavilion which could be used as a ballroom. It abutted on to the supremely snobbish headquarters of the Royal Yacht Squadron, who wanted it as a ladies' annexe. This was a vital necessity for the RYS and Commander Heckstall-Smith in his book, *Sacred Cowes*, satirically underlines its importance:

'While for more than a century the courteous and chivalrous gentlemen of the Squadron had enjoyed entertaining their ladies upon the lawn, none of them appears to have given a thought to their creature comforts, for, not to put too fine a point on the matter, there was no accommodation of any sort for ladies within the gates. But, so far as one knows, this point entirely escaped the notice of members until that particular afternoon in 1924 when the first woman set foot on the lawn in trousers for the first time. Then it was argued that if women went sailing in trousers but were not allowed to enter the precincts of the Squadron wearing them, reason and modesty decreed that accommodation must be provided where the forbidden garments could be discreetly removed.'

So, with Castle Rock in mind as lavatory and disrobing room, and with its ballroom a further plus factor, the Squadron started bidding – only to find an anonymous buyer in the market, bidding hard against them. It is very difficult to know exactly why Rosa decided to challenge them, for her eventual victory meant paying a high price for the property. It could well have been nostalgia for her days on the Kaiser's yacht; it could have been an original feud against some member of the Squadron who had erred in some way at the Cavendish; it could have been boredom. Out of the three, the last seems most likely.

So it was to the considerable dismay and irritation of the committee when it was learnt that they hadn't just been pipped at the post by an outsider but by the notorious Mrs Rosa Lewis. With great condescension Rosa leased the ballroom to them, although where the ladies removed their offending trousers at that time remains a mystery. So yet another country Cavendish was opened, and the young bloods of the age were given an opportnity to let rip at Cowes. Actresses and elder peers also came to Castle Rock, roulette was introduced as a diversion, and the RYS soon was made uncomfortably aware of their raffish neighbour. Even worse from the committee's point of view, less stuffy members of the RYS left their clubhouse for Rosa's Cowes Cavendish and such figures as Lord Birkenhead and Henry Denison were to be seen playing roulette there.

But worse still from the point of view of the Squadron was Rosa's insistence on conducting a personal feud with them. This makes one wonder if there were not certain central people on the committee who had been in the old Edward VII set and who had done her some disservice. Perhaps the physical crumbling of Edwardiana, and the bitterness she still felt over how she had been used as a discreet *concierge* and made to marry for respectability's sake, were the underlying reasons. Nevertheless, for whatever motive, Rosa certainly gave them hell and many a distinguished old sea-dog must have been reduced to near-apoplexy – and the younger members of the club to prayers that the verdant turf of the club lawns would swallow them, as she loudly commented on their love-life.

Apart from writing the Squadron a number of rude letters, she threatened them with legal action when they ineffectively tried to build lavatories on the lawns near the ballroom. She would also sit outside Castle Rock drinking champagne and, with a good view of the Squadron's activities, make a large number of extremely embarassing remarks. These often referred to members' lovers, members' personalities or members' physical appearance. She was unpredictable, foul-mouthed and a source of continuous horror to the Squadron. Many of the committee were so relieved when she wasn't at Castle Rock for the week-end that they must have felt like bringing out the champagne themselves.

Although in some ways Rosa's insulting behaviour at Cowes was debunking and funny, it was also hurtful and cruel, particularly as it was almost impossible to hit back at her. What is more, Rosa's public behaviour was becoming more and more extrovert, aggressive and insensitive. In the not too distant future she was to be removed from many public places and even those fondest of her fought shy of taking her out publicly. There was a raucous bitterness in her – a loneliness that Edith was not able to dispel entirely. A yearning to be loved – as her 'boys' had loved her during the First World War. And that yearning was to increase and to be reflected in her behaviour. It was only Edith and Maud who were to escape her tongue, and who could provide the stability that Rosa so desperately needed.

But it was not just the Royal Yacht Squadron who set the pace in Cowes. Rosa also set it, particularly when Poppy Baring was around. Poppy's appearances had the legendary quality of putting a voguish seal on the start of the social activities – if not the sailing. Her parents, Sir Godfrey and Lady Baring, who had a house at Cowes, point-blank forbade their daughter to visit Castle Rock, and so of course she used to go there as much as possible – with discretion. The Prince of Wales and Prince George often stayed with the Barings, who were obviously terrified that they would lose their royal privilege if the 'nefarious' visits of their daughter to Mrs Lewis's establishment were revealed.

Although Cowes was not then in its heyday (which had been pre-war) it was still a glamorous little spot. The King regarded his appearances there as a pleasant enough duty and was often to be seen spanking across the Solent in the Royal Yacht *Victoria and Albert*, but Queen Mary found the whole affair a living bore and spent most of her time mooching around antique shops. Rather bitterly, Rosa realized that she had come to Cowes too late. In Edward's time the place had been infinitely more romantic, with the yachts of the Tsar and the Kaiser anchored in the Roads. Edward would have entertained his sparkling international company on the lawns of the Royal Yacht Squadron and Rosa could well have cooked the dinners, thus more effectively snubbing the committee than by her present childish behaviour. Nor would she have had to rely on Poppy Baring to liven things up. It was sad – Rosa had been to so many different places to cook for Edward, but never Cowes. And now she bitterly resented it. She was too late, and being too late was henceforward to become a familiar source of frustration for her.

The press paid its usual attention to Rosa in the early months of 1925. On 23 January the London edition of the *Daily Mail* carried a hilarious report of a court case arising out of an argument Rosa had had with two of her clients, in which she had seized their belongings and refused to return them. The whole unnecessary business was typical of Rosa's increasing militancy.

Rosa also strongly 'took against' Mary Lawton when her long interview was published in New York the same year. Once again, the *Daily Mail* pounced on the highly saleable subject of Mrs Lewis and on 24 February it published a long article from which the following has been extracted:

WORLD-FAMOUS COOK
MRS ROSA LEWIS AND A U.S. BOOK 'A TRAVESTY'
'THE QUEEN OF COOKS – AND SOME KINGS'

'The story of Rosa Lewis, Cook Extraordinary and friend of the Royalty and Aristocracy of Europe.

A literary turmoil which may be taken to the law courts of the United States for settlement has been caused by the publication in America of a book with the above title, and the prompt and emphatic repudiation of its contents by the woman whose life story it purports to describe. The woman is Mrs Rosa Lewis, the proprietress of the Cavendish Hotel, Jermyn Street, S.W. i., who began to earn her livelihood at the age of 12 and won world-wide fame as a cook, sought after by royalty and Society to prepare dinners. . . .

The rejection by Mrs Lewis of the 60,000 words of tittle-tattle regarding people still alive and comment on the morals of present-day Society and celebrities which have been put into her mouth is contained in the following statement by her to a *Daily Mail* reporter.

"The book is a travesty. Miss Lawton on her arrival from America sought to obtain information from me and my staff.

One day I took compassion on her and gave a few harmless facts for the purpose of a short magazine article.

I learned that while I was on a visit to Norway, typists, book-keepers and personal servants who had been in my service were approached by her, and well-known Americans, who are among my friends, were canvassed extensively.

Numerous cables of protest against the preparation of a book in such circumstances were sent to the publishers and Miss Lawton, but they were disregarded. I received a cheque and immediately returned it." '

It would appear that the naïve Mary Lawton probably acted in good faith and that Rosa was merely ashamed of what she had said.

One of the most popular and sought after models of the early twenties was Chiquita, who told me that she regarded the Cavendish as a 'gorgeous boozy nursery' in which no one aged. 'Old people were considered fun and nothing was ever unpleasant.' It was only on emergence into the chill outside world that age again became unpleasantly relevant. Chiquita, one of the most striking models of the age, used to go to the Cavendish with the painter Guevara, who was later to paint Rosa. A close friend of Augustus John and his family, Chiquita also found in her Cavendish set the Tennants, Margot Asquith, Hermione Baddeley, Evan Morgan – all having fun and keeping everything light. Chiquita said: 'Rosa had a curious accent – rather aristocratic, with conscious working-class expletives breaking through. All servants at that time tended vocally to imitate their employers and Rosa was no different. But because she was so assertive and so individualistic she was determined to remind you about her real roots – and she brought the idioms in on purpose. She had a personality that perhaps is best described as rather grandly coarse!'

'At the time most of us were very young, but we all pretended to be very grown up. We smoked our cigarettes out of long holders and wore tight skirts with slits up the side and coloured knee length stockings – silk of course.'

Chiquita remembers the Cavendish in the early twenties as a gloriously unpredictable world of drinks and sudden parties. There was a faded elegance to it and the rooms were full of carefully arranged flowers. The atmosphere was one of an Edwardian country-house (smarter now since Edith's arrival) and Rosa would receive Chiquita and her friends in her parlour, quite often rather oddly sitting with her feet in a bowl of water. Moon was the man-servant of the times and he well maintained the high standard of decrepitude that people had come to expect from Rosa's front-of-house servants. It was Moon who was asked by Edith, who in turn had been commanded by Rosa, to turn away unwanted guests.

The streets near the Cavendish, remembers Chiquita, had a specific twenties smell to them – a mixture of richness and strength which would always stay in her memory. The fragrant aroma of Bond Street, the flowers in Berkeley Square, burnished leather shoes, brushed cloth, the garlic and sweat and cheap perfume of the stall women in Covent Garden, steaming manure, coffee beans roasting, and the hot smell of the pubs. Images, too – the flower girls around Eros and the Monico, messenger-boys running the streets, sandwich-board men, little boys in Fleet Street who would shovel up the fresh horse manure, barrel organs, bands, lone street musicians, the black, dark-green or yellow taxis – and then the hallway of the Cavendish 'full of luggage, the large central table bearing its load of neatly folded newspapers, and the rest of the space littered with abandoned tennis rackets and polo sticks. The furniture was dark and left no impression but the smell of beeswax did. Moon was always there.

. . . He used to sit in a sort of leather sentry box asleep, or only pretending to be asleep as he had to be on duty all day and night but I'm sure he was happy in a miserable sort of way . . . Rosa was usually sitting in her high-back chair, sometimes very well dressed but usually in a dressing-gown and bedroom slippers, with fur round them. When she went out she used just to throw a rather ancient fur coat over her shoulders.' But Chiquita also remembers that, despite Rosa's unconventional attire, she still had the most beautiful skin which seemed miraculously untouched by the late hours she kept.

Hardly any meals were cooked now at the Cavendish and most guests had them sent in. The letter-rack was bursting with letters 'to be sent on' and the hotel was seen as a poste restante for a seemingly homeless population of celebrities. The hall was stacked with luggage (some of it never claimed and dating back many years) and there were throngs of Americans. The hotel was fast becoming a sanctuary – a unique, informal and 'exclusive' club which had one enormous advantage, its timelessness. It was as if Rosa had cast the spell by deliberately rejecting change, by continuing to dress as an Edwardian 'lady'. She was now running a decadent Peter Pan world in which, psychologically at least, her citizens never grew up.

SIX

The Bright Young Things
1926–39

'Would you like to sin
On a tiger-skin,
With Elinor Glyn?
Or would you prefer
To err
On another fur?'

BY THIS STAGE ROSA HAD DEVELOPED A MODEST BROCHURE
for the Cavendish. It read:

Cavendish Hotel
St. James's, S.W. 1
This well-known and old-established Family Hotel has now
been re-decorated throughout, and fitted with every modern
convenience and requirement, including the installation of a
telephone in each sitting room. Suites of rooms are also provided
with private bathrooms attached. The rooms are steam-heated
and lighted by electric light, and there are lifts for the convenience of visitors. All the bedrooms look out upon a charming
square open courtyard, and have thus the great boon of quietude,
although in the heart of fashionable St James's. The Cavendish is
centrally situated in the best part of London, being near Hyde
Park, Rotten Row, Regent Street, Bond Street, and St. James's
Street, and within easy distance of the Clubs and theatres.
The Cavendish is noted for the excellency of its cuisine, the
Proprietress being also a very successful society caterer.

In addition to the Hotel accommodation, there are a number
of fully furnished Flats for Bachelors, containing Sitting Room,
one or two Bedrooms and Bathroom. There is a private
entrance in Duke Street, W., also direct access to the Hotel.
The rates for these Flats are very moderate.

Estimates given for Receptions, Dinners, Balls, etc.

MOTOR SERVICE
There is run by the Hotel a service of Motor Cars, including
Rolls-Royces and Daimlers.

Visitors can arrange at any moment to avail themselves of
these Cars at very moderate rates.

Special inclusive charge for Dinner, Theatre and return.

Cars and Buses meet all trains.

Garage and Parking Space for Cars at rear with direct access to the Hotel.

The Manager will be pleased to quote Special Rates by the Day, Week or Month.

Owing to the difficulty in getting washing returned promptly, we have installed a fully equipped MODERN LAUNDRY in the Hotel, and have made arrangements for visitors to have their washing returned in 24 hours upon notice being given when handed to our staff.

FINE HAND-WORK A SPECIALITY

The brochure included alluring advertisements for both Castle Rock and The Homestead:

'CASTLE ROCK', COWES, ISLE OF WIGHT

Delightful old country house standing in lovely gardens and containing 14 bedrooms, 2 bathrooms, 3 reception rooms and usual domestic offices.

Charmingly and comfortably furnished.

Situated on Sea Front adjoining Royal Yacht Squadron.

Ideal position for Cowes week and the Yachting season.

Telephone: Cowes 95.

For terms apply:

Mrs. Rosa Lewis, CAVENDISH HOTEL.

'THE HOMESTEAD', JEVINGTON, SUSSEX

Delightful old country house situated on the South Downs, only 2½ miles from Eastbourne and under two hours from London by road.

It contains: 7 bedrooms, bathroom, 3 reception rooms and the usual offices. Central Heating, Telephone, Electric Light, every comfort and convenience. Beautifully furnished.

Excellent detached Garage for 3 or 4 cars with 4 rooms and bath over.

Charming old world gardens including tennis and croquet lawns, flower and kitchen gardens, greenhouses, etc., in all nearly 8 acres.

Telephone: Hampden Park 7.

For terms apply:

Mrs. Rosa Lewis,

CAVENDISH HOTEL

The phenomenon of the Bright Young Things was both vacuous and irritating to most people, except of course the Bright Young Things and Mrs Rosa Lewis. They saved her from becoming moribund and she happily accepted her role as a somewhat doubtful parent to the awesome pace of their gaiety. By 1926, Rosa was fifty-nine, and playing hostess to their many activities.

Meanwhile, London night-life was buzzing away, usually 'gone on to' after drinks at the Cavendish, though the Licensing Act of 1921 had made severe restrictions on drinking activities. No drinks could be served without food after eleven and glasses had to be removed from the tables at midnight. To overcome these problems the night spots became clubs, which had the easiest to join membership lists in the country. The secretary would instantly propose you and the commissionaire was a willing seconder. Nevertheless, the clubs were still continually raided by the police and much aristocratic embarrassment was caused. Champagne, selling at the Cavendish at about 12s. 6d. a bottle was double that price in the night clubs and possibly treble during the hours of illegal drinking. Indeed so much profit was made that magistrate's fines were not considered very important. Tougher restrictions came in, however, and in 1924 the queen of all night club owners, Mrs Kate Meyrick (who ran the 43 Club and the Silver Slipper Club amongst others) was sentenced to six months in Holloway. The same crowd moved from club to club, favouring one or the other until fashion dictated a move.

The political situation in the first five years of the twenties did not bode well. Industrial unrest had begun in 1919, prices soared and were not matched by wages in 1920, and by 1921 the economy was going downhill fast. The answer was seen to be drastic government cuts, but when carried out, they were not drastic enough. Only sixty-four million pounds were saved as opposed to the recommended cuts of seventy-five million. In 1922 the coalition government fell and the Conservatives were returned to power under the leadership of Bonar Law, who was Prime Minister for only seven months, resigning on grounds of ill-health. Baldwin replaced him in May 1925. Disillusionment had already set in, particularly among the ex-servicemen. Had they fought so hard for poverty? For redundancy? For near-starvation? Apparently they had.

The Bright Young Things were an ironic contrast to all this. One of their most obsessive jollities was the treasure hunt, which would often start from Piccadilly Circus, the Cavendish or Horse Guards Parade, and end up in such far-flung in-spots as Maidenhead or Bray. Originally devised by Lady Eleanor and Loelia Ponsonby, the treasure hunts would start at 2 am and the participants would spend all night driving around in their cars, looking for clues. Lady Diana Cooper was also an inveterate treasure-hunter and wrote in her book *The Light of Common Day*, 'Treasure hunts were dangerous and scandalous, but there was no sport to touch them. A clue might lead to a darkened city street, there to find a lady in distress, with a dead duellist at her feet, who would hand the next clue through her tears. This might lead to a far plague-spot where a smallpoxed ghost would whisper a conundrum that took you to a mare's nest in Kensington Gardens, and thence to a Chinese puzzle in Whitechapel.' All this heady and romantic activity was brought down to earth with the more mundane but pleasantly vulgar scavenger hunts. Almost impossible objects had to be found at night, such as horseshoes, lifebuoys and boaters. The very last item on the list had to be something unique – and Lady Diana Cooper remembers Michael Herbert's producing 'a coutil-busked corset belonging to Mrs Lewis of the Cavendish Hotel, signed, cross-signed and under-signed with the names, quips and quizzes of her noble and notable clients'. Quite how Rosa came to part with this hallowed object is far from clear!

Hoaxes were another pastime. The irrepressible Lady Eleanor, for instance, had a number of cards printed with the legend 'Miss Babington Gooch, Amalgamated Provincial Press' and proceeded to conduct a number of spoof interviews with luckless celebrities staying in expensive London hotels. Another idea was to organize a fake modern art exhibition in a Bond Street Gallery, which showed the advanced work of 'Bruno Hatt, the German artist'. They tipped off the *Express* and reporters arrived to watch some of the distinguished guests at the private view walk into some nasty traps. Winston Churchill didn't, deeming the show to be 'bloody rubbish'. Margot Asquith did, and worsened her position by giving the reporters a brisk lecture on the evaluation of modern art.

Parties were thrown in ABC tea-shops, or alternatively on buses, trains or tubes. Other parties occurred – Russian parties, Greek parties, colour parties, circus parties, baby parties, and – most shocking of all – bottle parties. Waugh's *Vile Bodies* best epitomizes the feeling of the older generation towards the Bright Young Things:

'The topic of the Younger Generation spread through the company like a yawn. Royalty remarked on their absence and those happy mothers who had even one docile daughter in two swelled with pride and commiseration.

"I'm told that they're having another of their parties," said Mrs Mouse, "in an aeroplane this time".

"In an aeroplane? How very extraordinary."

"Of course, I never hear a word from Mary, but her maid told my maid . . ."

"What I always wonder, Kitty dear, is what they actually *do* at these parties of theirs. I mean, *do* they . . . ?"

"My dear, from all I hear, I think they do."

"Oh, to be young again, Kitty. When I think, my dear, of all the trouble and exertion which we had to go through to be even moderately bad . . . those passages in the early morning and mama sleeping next door."

"And yet, my dear, I doubt very much whether they really *appreciate* it all as much as we should . . . young people take things so much for granted. *Si la jeunesse savait.*"

"*Si la vieillesse pouvait*, Kitty." '

Gatecrashing was very much the rage at the Bright Young Things' parties although some parties were more amusing to gatecrash than others, particularly when one could avoid dressing up and *still* arrive uninvited at, say, the Babies' Ball. Guests arrived at this in prams and became very drunk, dressed in a variety of sailor-suits, rompers and pinafores. The invitations for these parties read: 'We are having Romps from ten o'clock to bedtime. Do write and say you'll come, and we'll love to have Nanny too. Pram-park provided. Dress: anything from birth to school age.' Other 'ripping' ideas included other forms of fancy dress parties where for instance Mrs Dudley Ward arrived dressed as a little girl and departed in a donkey costume, Lord Blandford (later to become the Duke of Marlborough) appeared as a female Channel-swimmer, the Prince of Wales came attired in full Ku-Klux-Klan regalia, Duff Cooper as one of the three blind mice, Lady Louis Mountbatten as a white ostrich, and Lord Berners as a monkey-bride. Certainly an all-star cast of the surreal.

Other activities involved Murder parties, Russian parties, 'Follow-my-leader' through Selfridge's, and Pyjama and Bottle parties. Of the latter the *Daily News* wrote: 'The bottles of refreshments which the guests were expected to bring provided an amusing distraction. There was hair-restorer, distilled water, beer, ink, petrol, Ethyl, smelling-salts, Thames water, Jordan water, cabbage water, and water from a pool alive with tadpoles.'

Some of the wildest parties, particularly those held by the Aly Khan in association with a leading jockey, Michael Beary, were naturally held at the Cavendish and Rosa's parlour echoed to the jargon of the times. 'Too perfectly amazing', 'too grisly for words', 'too tired-making' and 'too sick-making' were amongst the most popular expressions.

There was also, of course, the dancing craze which very much dominated the twenties. There were plenty of venues for it, ranging from tea-dances to dinner dances, to floors in night clubs and restaurants. Paul Whiteman played and the Criterion Roof, Romano's, the Savoy, the Hammersmith Palais and Prince's also echoed to the jazz age.

Much boosted by a scandalized press and later much discussed by Lord Castlerosse's gossip column in the *Express*, the smart young set got considerably more mileage out of their activities than was merited. It is unlikely, however, that their morals were any worse than the Edwardians' and there was certainly no press-created personality cult in Edwardian times. Sex was still romantic and superficial 'love' was used as a reason for having it. Girls were 'good scouts', 'good chaps'. Sometimes they were 'plucky' and occasionally they were 'just like brothers'. Unlike the Victorians, and to a lesser extent the Edwardians, the Bright Young Things did not patronize the poor and the gathering unrest, leading up to the shock of the General Strike in 1926, was ignored. This attitude is best expressed by Loelia Ponsonby's comment, 'From time to time I wrote cheerfully in my diary that we seemed to be on the brink of a bloody revolution, but it was a possibility that had been in the back of the minds of the upper classes ever since the days of Marie Antoinette and which they had got quite used to, so in the next sentence I went on to describe how I was trimming a hat or arranging a dinner party.' As for Sidney and Beatrice Webb, the Fabian Society and Bernard Shaw – they were ludicrous cranks quite beyond the pale.

One of Rosa's most devoted admirers and friends was the high-living Daphne Vivian, who was later to be the Marchioness of Bath until she was divorced and became Daphne Fielding. In her book about Rosa Lewis, *The Duchess of Jermyn Street*, she describes how, on summer's nights in 1923, her own particular herd of Bright Young Things would pile into taxis and set out for the Cavendish. Moon, the irascible night porter, would grudgingly let them in and they would all rush into Rosa's inner sanctum. To them she was 'just the thing' of the moment – a classic eccentric who specialized in licentious or 'awful' remarks. To her they were her 'boys' back again – and 'girls' too. Her own. Amongst Rosa's extended family were Daphne Vivian herself, Harry Weymouth (her husband-to-be), Nancy Mitford, Elizabeth Ponsonby, Mark Ogilvie Grant, Martin Wilson (Lord Ribblesdale's grandson), Brian Howard (the classic Waugh figure), David and Olivia Plunket Greene, Lettice Lygon (Lord Beauchamp's daughter) and many other aristocratic names. Not only did they find Rosa 'the thing', but so were many of her more oddly assorted guests. Using grisly stage cockney but no doubt accurately reflecting how Rosa would play up to the role required of her, Mrs Fielding relates a typical scene: 'Rosa flings open the door. "Here they all are. There's Snivelling Dick . . . knew him before he was born. Pots of money. They gave him a gold cigarette case when his trousers fell down in Piccadilly. Young Evan's upstairs having twins. Lady What's-er-name over there looks like a tart but she isn't. Edith and I stopped her brother marrying that gingerbust. Queen Mary thinks the world of her." '

Poor Rosa – her Bright Young Things were not to sparkle for long. They grew up and although many of them remained loyal to her, it was their youth that she wanted.

It's easy enough to be contemptuous of this young set and their self-centredness but they really had very little reason to behave otherwise. Like any 'younger generation' group they were reacting against the values of the older generation and this is a depressing and sheep-like cycle that will continue for all time. But it must be made clear that the Bright Young Things had a damned sight more to resent than many of their successors. The stuffiness of their upper-class mentors, the Season, etiquette, obedience, the press – everything was there to encourage them to react as outrageously as possible against the fierce system that attempted to govern their lives.

Evelyn Waugh's description of Rosa in *Vile Bodies* is, in a sense, all she deserved, for her outward manner was very much like his characterization. The book didn't appear until 1930 but Lottie Crump is very much Rosa of her Bright Young Thing period. Waugh was an *habitué* of the Cavendish but not a permanent member of the group surrounding her by any means. Rosa was not only infuriated by Waugh's description of herself but also his use of the name of the *maître d'hôtel* of the Cavendish as the social-climbing horror, Archie Stewart. Christopher Sykes, in his biography of Waugh, says, 'Rosa used to screech in rage: "There are two bastards I'm not going to have in this house, one is that rotten little Donegall and the other is that little swine Evelyn Waugh." ' In fact she was obviously very hurt by the Lottie Crump description and Waugh was thoroughly insensitive to have made the character so very like her, as the following extract will show:

'Lottie Crump, proprietress of Shepheard's Hotel, Dover Street, attended invariably by two Cairn terriers, is a happy reminder to us that the splendours of the Edwardian era were not entirely confined to Lady Anchorage or Mrs Blackwater. She is a fine figure of a woman, singularly unscathed by any sort of misfortune and superbly oblivious of those changes in the social order which agitate the more observant *grandes dames* of her period. When the war broke out she took down the signed photograph of the Kaiser and, with some solemnity, hung it in the men-servants' lavatory; it was her one combative action; since then she has had her worries – income-tax forms and drink restrictions and young men whose fathers she used to know, who give her bad cheques, but these have been soon forgotten; one can go to Shepheard's parched with modernity any day, if Lottie likes one's face, and still draw up, cool and uncontaminated, great healing draughts from the well of Edwardian certainty.

Shepheard's has a plain, neatly pointed brick front and large, plain doorway. Inside it is like a country house. Lottie is a great one for sales, and likes, whenever one of the great houses of her day is being sold up, to take away something for old times' sake. There is a good deal too much furniture at Shepheard's, some of it rare, some of it hideous beyond description; there is plenty of red plush and red morocco and innumerable wedding presents of the 'eighties; in particular many of those massive, mechanical devices covered with crests and monograms, and associated in some way with cigars. It is the sort of house in which one expects to find croquet mallets and polo sticks in the bathroom, and children's toys at the bottom of one's chest of drawers, and an estate map and an archery target – exuding straw – and a bicycle and one of those walking-sticks which turn into saws, somewhere in passages, between baize doors, smelling of damp. (As a matter of fact, all you are likely to find in your room at Lottie's is an empty champagne bottle or two and a crumpled camisole.)

The servants, like the furniture, are old and have seen aristocratic service. Doge, the head waiter, who is hard of hearing, partially blind, and tortured with gout, was once a Rothschild's butler. He had, in fact, on more than one occasion in Father Rothschild's youth, dandled him on his knee, when he came with his father (at one time fifteenth richest man in the world) to visit his still richer cousins, but it would be unlike him to pretend that he ever really liked the embryo Jesuit who was 'too clever by half', given to asking extraordinary questions, and endowed with a penetrating acumen in the detection of falsehood and exaggeration.

Besides Doge, there are innumerable old housemaids always trotting about with cans of hot water and clean towels. There is also a young Italian who does most of the work and gets horribly insulted by Lottie, who once caught him powdering his nose, and will not let him forget it. Indeed, it is one of the few facts in Lottie's recent experience that seems always accessible.

Lottie's parlour, in which most of the life of Shepheard's

centres, contains a comprehensive collection of signed photographs. Most of the male members of the royal families of Europe are represented (except the ex-Emperor of Germany, who has not been reinstated, although there was a distinct return of sentiment towards him on the occasion of his second marriage). There are photographs of young men on horses riding in steeplechases, of elderly men leading in the winners of 'classic' races, of horses alone and of young men alone, dressed in tight, white collars or in the uniform of the Brigade of Guards. There are caricatures by 'Spy', the photographs cut from illustrated papers, many of them with brief obituary notices 'killed in action'. There are photographs of yachts in full sail and of elderly men in yachting caps; there are some funny pictures of the earliest kind of motor-car. There are very few writers or painters and no actors, for Lottie is true to the sound old snobbery of pound sterling and strawberry leaves.'

The hotel was now running on full staff again, its fortunes were improving, and Edith had managed the massive job of refurbishing the curtains and fittings. The atmosphere was still very much more that of a club than a hotel and its staff continued to reflect a mood of some antiquity and eccentricity. One such character was Steffany, who died in the mid-twenties and looked as if he should have died many years before. He was deaf, almost blind and performed haltingly as a general factotum. Shane Leslie described him in his novel, *The Anglo-Catholic*, as follows: 'His white mottled face bore the expression of a gargoyle and his skull seemed to be fringed with cobweb. His back was bent like Diogenes in a tub. He moved with great ponderous dignity for if Ganymede, the cupbearer of the Gods, was his spiritual forefather, his grandmother might well have been the Dowager Empress of China.'

By now Rosa had become more inactive. She seemed content to be the central figure of a unique environment. This is not to say that she did not administer the staff but it was in a charismatic, mother-figure style, whilst Edith did the book-keeping and more common or garden organization. Rosa had a rough kindness to the staff although it was not without a certain bullying quality which probably sprang from her own past experience and her great ability to be a good cook *and* a good kitchen manager. Rosa spread her patronage to surrounding businesses such as tailors' and flower shops and their trade naturally boomed as she persuaded some of her richer clients to use them. What her richer clients did not use, however, were the local prostitutes, although Rosa knew most of them by name. Moreover she patronized them with a gift at Christmas. But there her involvement with them ended, for the girls she procured for her Cavendish clients were strictly clean and therefore mostly amateur. Rosa was aware that no responsible, if not entirely respectable, hotel proprietor should risk spreading venereal disease around the premises.

By the middle of the twenties there was an acceptance of the vast changes brought about by the 1914–18 war and it was further acknowledged that the 'wrong' people had the money. Nevertheless the London season was still continuing, more or less intact, and its activities were reflected by such glossy journals as *The Bystander*, *The Tatler*, and *Sporting and Dramatic*. Domestic servants were still obtainable but would demand an 'all found' situation. Meanwhile women's fashions had dropped the frills and fripperies of the early twenties and become much more severe and stark. Bobbed or 'Eton-cropped' hair was covered by the ghastly cloche hat, stockings were silk or cotton or wool, and after 1925 the skirt shot up to above the knee.

Men's fashions were more conservative with hair strictly short-back-and-sides. Off-duty wear was still Oxford bags, co-respondent's shoes, jolly ties and light-coloured suits. But these, of course, could not possibly be worn as office-wear and this was either the deadly conventional suit or the black jacket, black and white striped trousers, umbrella and bowler hat.

Emancipation of a kind was growing but it was obviously very limited. Educated, middle-class women took jobs and spent their earnings on clothes, drink and cigarettes. Smoking was not acceptable in public and whilst their aristocratic and upper-middle-class peers swarmed round the highspots of London, the middle classes imitated them by driving in open sports cars, limping from one cocktail party to another, and trying to appear as 'wicked' as possible.

On 3 May 1926 the General Strike was called and many of the Cavendish set turned out to do their 'duty' as emergency drivers, signalmen, tea brewers, and so on. Basically it was the climax of an industrial unrest that had been tinder-dry for years. Prices and unemployment were high, there was a serious housing shortage and, in July 1925, the Conservative Government announced that it was going to discontinue its subsidy to the coal-mining industry. As a result the employers declared that they would slash wages, lengthen working hours and do away with minimum wage principles. A Government Commission largely agreed with the employers' attitude – and from that moment on the General Strike was a *fait accompli*.

Ethel Mannin wrote about the crisis of the General Strike in her autobiography *Young in the Twenties*:

> 'By the middle of the decade some of the grim realities began to impinge on the fun; some of the muddy water of the rising tide of misery and despair in the industrial north, where mass unemployment made a bitter mockery of the jubilant war-time promise of a 'land fit for heroes to live in' when it was all over, began to seep through to the south. . . . For years we had been singing, as we cavorted round the floor at tea-dances, the dinner-dances, the supper-dances, the night-clubs '*It ain't gonna rain no mo', no mo', it ain't gonna rain no mo'*', but now it was raining hard; pelting; coming down whole water. Even in London we knew it; the General Strike caused a good deal of inconvenience . . .'

But Lady Diana Cooper, despite the fact that she was sure she could hear 'the tumbrils rolling and heads sneezing into the baskets' kept cool and used her car as a taxi. C. E. Pitman, the Oxford stroke, drove a train, the headmaster of Eton and dozens of his assistant masters became special constables, Edwina Mountbatten and the Hon. Mrs Richard Norton manned the *Express*'s switchboards. To most of the Bright Young Things it was all a tremendous lark: many a cloche hat was seen behind the canteen counter, and many a Fair Isle sweater and plus fours on the footplate or in the signal boxes. All the stout-hearted girls and boys were out to beat the reds and the strike. And indeed when it finally ended there were regretful feelings among the Bright Young Things, who had temporarily discovered that being useful for once was just 'the thing'.

Some months later Rosa and Edith, also feeling the economic pinch, departed to America on a rather curious sales trip. She had acquired as an IOU some enormous tapestries which illustrated scenes from the life of Constantine the Great, drawn in the Rubens style and reputed to be Gobelins. If they were genuine, they would obviously fetch a good price in New York and Rosa was anxious to get rid of them.

Her welcome in New York was tremendous and this, if nothing else, must have made her realize what a renowned public figure she had become. All the ex-guests of the Cavendish ensured she was shown the sights, black market prohibition-busting drink greeted them at their Ritz-Carlton suite and there were over two-hundred telegrams. The press interviewed her on a number of subjects, but many of them concentrated on Edward VII and the food he had most liked. In a resultant *Colliers* article Rosa discussed the eating habits of the current Prince of Wales, although it is unlikely that she had ever met him and certainly never cooked for him. She told the reporter: 'The present Prince of Wales will eat almost anything you give him whether it is good for him or not but he is given to worrying about taking on a bit of flesh. I took him in hand about it, "Your health comes first" I told him, "what if you are a bit stoutish? Your grandfather was, and a splendid gentleman he was, if you don't mind." '

In fact the current Prince of Wales was a willowy figure but Rosa can be forgiven her made-up anecdote. The last thing she would have wanted to do would be to appear out of the swim – an elderly woman who had once consorted with the fathers of the famous. If royalty didn't want to know her now – well, she would have to pretend that they did! Luckily when it came to appraising cooking and eating habits on both sides of the Atlantic she was on safer and more truthful ground. She told the *New York Times* that she approved of American meat but that she didn't like the idea of serving chops with 'a sauce and kidney trimmings'. Instead 'a grilled chop should stand or fall on the flavour imported by its own juice which makes it succulent, delicious and epicurean.'

Some of Rosa's exaggerations to the American press could be more hilarious than pathetic and in the *Colliers* article she relates the amazing story of the eating energies of the anonymous Lady B. 'The greatest eater I have ever seen was Lady B. Law! how that woman could eat. She was as big as a house – a large house, mind you – and it was nothing for her to eat a five-pound fowl stuffed with truffles, not to speak of the soup and a river pike stuffed and smothered in a cream of prawns and a salad. But she did it with an air which lent a beautiful air of delicacy to what might have been a gastronomic shambles.' The last comment is reassuring – at least the prodigious (if largely fictitious) eater was not breaking wind after each course.

The *New Yorker* in its 'The Talk of the Town' column of 22 January 1927, commented wryly on Rosa's activities in New York.

'It seems that Mrs Rosa Lewis, known somewhat sweepingly as the Queen of Cooks, has met many sad-faced old preterists who have been gathering each day at her suite in the Ritz to recall the menus of her great dinners served in the day when Victoria's naughty son was her most lavish patron. Mrs Lewis divides her time between such reminiscences, it is said, and a frantic search of the telephone book for the numbers of those persons who might be able to purchase the $3,000,000 tapestries she has brought, and when she failed to find Otto Khan, Marcus Loew or the Cathedral of St John the Divine in the alphabetical lists she burst into the vehemence of billingsgate.

She came over in the imperial suite of the *Berengaria*; and, finding no cabs at the dock, is said to have hailed a passing limousine with three young men inside, requesting that she be allowed to sit on a lap as far as the Ritz. She got the lap, largely because one of the young bloods recognized her as the proprietor of the Hotel Cavendish in London, out of which he had been thrown no less than four times.'

The *New Yorker* concludes on an even more ironic note:

. . . Into her stay here she has crowded many things. She has learned Southern recipes from a negro cook, and the secret of graceful old age from Chauncey Depew; she has acquired an unbelievable appetite for clams, and has reviewed the West Point cadets. But apparently she has one or two things still to learn. The other day, for instance, she held up a bottle of gin which had been presented to her, with the remark: "Oh, this must be good – it has a Gordon label." '

Unfortunately the main object of the journey, the sale of the supposed Gobelins, was never achieved, for they turned out to be fakes. Rosa and Edith returned after three weeks, the tapestries still with them. But Rosa was not depressed. She had loved every moment of the New York trip: it had made the adrenalin surge in her – as well as the champagne – and she came back to England a revitalized woman.

So Rosa returned to the Cavendish, its Bright Young Things and the last few years of the twenties. It is worth pausing at this point to include a couple of cameos of Rosa and the Cavendish drawn by their clients in the mid-twenties. The first was contributed to Rosa's original biographer, Michael Harrison, by P. A. Ennor:

'I am one of what must be a large number of my generation who, as young men, used to visit the Cavendish Hotel in the late 20s and early 30s.

I remember Rosa Lewis, her old companion, Edith, and venerable waiter, Stefani, well; and also the white West Highland dogs that Rosa used always to have.

The most interesting room in the hotel was the one on the right-hand side of the front-door. The walls of this were literally covered with photographs – mostly autographed – of sporting, social and Service personalities of the late Victorian and Edwardian epochs.

Alas, most of these photographs were lost or damaged in the last war. They provided a most interesting and historical record of the age and way of life they covered.

Though much was Victorian, and the house itself, of course very much older, the whole atmosphere and tone was completely Edwardian.

It was in the room to which I refer that most of the life of the place was conducted, and where one went to 'have a drink' – which was invariably a bottle of champagne.'

Another shows Rosa in a more vicious mood. A Mr Forbes Cheston wrote:

'My father was the architect to Bethlem Hospital, who owned the freehold of the Cavendish (and my brother, Jack Cheston, afterwards) and Rosa adored them both. I knew her all my life, but she cordially detested me and my mother, and hadn't much use for my sister. I suppose the first time I remember seeing her was when the family stayed at the Cavendish, as Rosa's guests, and watched the coronation of George v, from a window in St James's Street. Very shortly after that, my parents' silver wedding dinner took place there, and, later, my sister's wedding reception. Rosa loudly designated the bridegroom's family as a lot of long-nosed frumps. She also made herself extremely popular at my brother's wedding – with everyone, that is, except the bride, whom she reduced to tears. We didn't like her much, either. She arrived at my father's funeral, unexpectedly, and rather tight, just as the cortège was leaving the house. (Hat on back-to-front and fur coat over a night-gown). She announced that she wouldn't go to the cemetery, but would have some whisky with Mother, who was five minutes ahead of hysterics. When we got back, Rosa had gone, and Mother was as angry as I ever saw her, but she would never tell us what transpired.'

Mr Cheston's sister, Mrs Hall, wrote a little wildly:

'I was in Mrs Lewis's sitting-room one night. I can't now remember the name of the room, but nobody went there unless they were personal friends of Mrs Lewis or invited by her. The room was crowded with men who were sitting all around, some on chairs but mostly on the floor; most of them pretty drunk. Then the door opened and another woman came in. Mrs Lewis looked at her, then smiled her charming smile, and said: "Ah, Sophie! Come in, Sophie, my dear!" Then she smiled round the room, and said: "You all know Sophie, don't you? Nice, clean 'arlot, aren't you, Sophie?" Sophie just smiled and came and sat down next to Mrs Lewis. Years, or may be only months, later (I can't remember) I recall Mrs Lewis coming into her room, very upset, as Sophie had died, and she had just returned from the funeral. She was very fond of Sophie, but I think she was distressed partly because Sophie, being a Jewess, had been buried standing up. Anyhow, that is what she told us.'

Rosa didn't behave unpredictably just in the Cavendish, she

was beginning to behave more and more unpredictably outside it. Largely she behaved badly because she needed to live up to her reputation as a 'character' – and 'characters' are never pleasant. Malcolm Muggeridge, knowing her many years later, shares my own inherent dislike of this kind of image projection. 'As it happens,' he wrote, 'I temperamentally find people who become "characters" unsympathetic. She did. And I thought, on the whole, rather a grasping, untruthful and unpleasant one.'

Maud Puckering, Edith Jeffrey's sister, thinks totally differently. She claims that Rosa, although sometimes inclined to goad, was a far more restrained character than the ex-clients of the Cavendish state. Maud never heard her swear or be vicious, and she has a number of alternative motives for Rosa's actions. The house at Jevington, she says, was not a second Cavendish but a private home into which Rosa took only her close personal friends. Castle Rock, Maud states, was bought by Rosa as a home for old Mrs Jeffrey – the mother of the two women who had become the only family Rosa now had. She also claims that Rosa never bought the property to abuse the Royal Yacht Squadron and never sat on any lawn (because it was not in viewing sight) to hurl insults at them.

The answer to this ambiguity would appear to be that Rosa never showed her 'other' side to Maud. Indeed she was rather multi-sided. To young women she could be patronizing or alternatively protective, earnestly advising them to 'get as much out of men as you could'. To young men she was either chaffing, belligerent or maternalistic. To older, isolated men she was always maternalistic. (Ribblesdale used to go shopping or for walks in the park with her when he was at his most despairing.) To older women, providing they were well-to-do, she tended, in the main, to be admiring. To servants she was either roughly rude or roughly kind. To prostitutes she seemed to regard herself as some kind of small-beer financial welfare agency. Towards her own parents and family she was negative. But with her surrogate family – Edith, Maud and their mother – she was definitely at her most genuine. Edith never married but Maud, after a spell as matron on the Cunard Line, married one of its employees and had three children. Rosa, like Edith, was not keen on young children but was certainly never unkind to them and became more pleasant to them as they grew up. There had developed a very strong bond between the three women, Rosa, Edith and Maud, and Rosa was at her most relaxed, most secure, if not at her most contented, with them. That's why she showed them the best side of her nature – the ordinary side. The one that didn't have to be acted out all the time.

It was boredom that motivated Rosa's unfortunate excursions into other establishments. One such victim was David Tennant's Gargoyle Club, whose members included Augustus John, Compton Mackenzie and A. P. Herbert amongst others. Perhaps it was its bohemian atmosphere that made Rosa take it on as a challenge, for not in the wildest imagination could the Cavendish be deemed to be bohemian. Perhaps, and more likely, it was the fact that the Gargoyle was a closed shop. She would ignore the rules, refused to be accompanied by a member – and also refused to sign the visitors' book. To David Tennant's horror she also brought her dog, Kippy, which was more than he could stand – despite the bohemianism of the atmosphere. However, Rosa had her come-uppance when she invaded Tennant's own flat on the premises which he and his second wife used from time to time. Daphne Fielding relates the story in her book, *The Duchess of Jermyn Street*: 'This had been recently decorated, and Rosa, like Queen Mary, always liked to inspect any domestic improvements. Virginia had a treasured collection of miniscule shells which she had displayed on a tray in a mosaic-like pattern. Feeling peckish and mistaking these for cocktail dainties, Rosa seized a handful, popped them into her mouth and began to crunch them between her teeth.'

But other establishments were less tolerant of her intrusions and as these continued through the late twenties and right through the thirties, the managements became more and more irritated. A case in point was the Savoy, a bastion of conservatism that became another of Rosa's victims. One of its former employees, anxious to remain anonymous, pointed out that she used to arrive alone and stroll around accosting the guests, many of whom, of course, were *habitués* of the Cavendish. However, the Savoy management of the time regarded the Cavendish as a most unsavoury place and were very uneasy about its popularity with many of their customers. But as if that wasn't enough, it was intolerable to have its proprietress, a lady of similarly doubtful reputation, parading around their premises, and making horrendous remarks to their clients, often loudly referring to their sexual escapades, their mistresses and their drunken exploits. At first the barmen were given instructions not to serve her with drinks. But this was not a sufficient deterrent and she continued to arrive on unpredictable occasions and fraternize all too intimately. Eventually the house detective was given the job of asking her to leave which, no doubt after a few well-chosen words, she did.

The rather *louche* reputation of the Cavendish continued to grow although it had an old-fashioned respectable reputation too, which mainly applied to country visitors and to the priests and bishops who, unaccountably, often stayed there. Perhaps it was the hotel's proximity to the famous church of St James that drew them there.

One of the best summaries of what was really happening at the Cavendish came from Seymour Leslie in his book, *The Jerome Connexion*:

> 'Returning from Bishra and Tunis, I motored down to Sussex with Rosa Lewis from her Cavendish Hotel. She began as my aunt Olive Guthrie's cook, then went to the Ribblesdales,* then opened her famous little 'hotel' in Jermyn Street, for which her critics have another name. She is obviously very highly 'protected' and must be useful to the police. She helps to 'initiate' young men from the best families (who have every confidence in her) so that they can sow their wild oats with the minimum of scandal. She is a great London character like Frau Sacher in Vienna. We took our hamper and she brought out caviare and 1906 Moet.'

The social round in the late twenties was a heavy one for Rosa and some of the personalities associated with her and the Cavendish are worth expanding on. In the background the resentment and suspicion brought about by the General Strike continued. From the aristocratic and upper-middle-class point of view there was a certain sense of loss after the ending of the strike and a cartoon in Punch showed an apathetic young man in a college blazer staring blankly out of the window whilst his mother says to a friend, 'You see, he misses the Strike so dreadfully.' An election was due in 1929 and both peace and employment were

* In fact she only cooked for them. [Author's note]

the main issues. The Conservatives claimed that unemployment was not as bad as was stated and their manifesto promised slum clearance, as well as welfare and education benefits. The state of the parties at this point was that Labour had 287 seats, the Conservatives had 261 seats and Liberals had 59 seats.

Social life continued to flourish and there seemed no threat from the future – only a feeling of bitterness and unrest that could now be ignored, since the workers and therefore the 'reds' had been crushed by the collapse of the Strike. Principal party-givers included Gordon Selfridge, who threw striking parties on the roof of his Oxford Street store with such guests as C. B. Cochran, Tallulah Bankhead, Lady Cunard – and of course Rosa Lewis. Seymour Leslie remembered that Gordon Selfridge also threw the most fantastic parties on General Election nights. About four thousand people crowded one floor of his department store. There were three ballrooms, two supper-rooms and an enormous hall showing computed results. The function would cost him about six thousand pounds, and apart from Rosa Lewis, there were dozens of celebrities including Charles Laughton, A. P. Herbert, Douglas Fairbanks, Barbara Hutton, Lady Plunkett, Madeleine Carroll and so on.

Lady Cunard was, of course, another principal hostess and both she and her daughter were *habitués* of the Cavendish. The American wife of Sir Bache Cunard, the grandson of the founder of the Cunard Line, she had run parties in Grosvenor Square that could be said to be of a 'salon' or 'café society' nature. She separated from him in 1911 after falling in love with Thomas Beecham and she later became a supporter of the international seasons of grand opera at Covent Garden. Stella Margetson writes in her book, *The Long Party*: 'The luncheon parties and dinner parties she gave round her circular dining table of lapis lazuli, which reflected the candlelight and the gilt epergne of naked nymphs and naiads standing at the centre of it, were staged with a perfection that enchanted everyone.' Lord Kinross wrote of her: 'As one switches the radio to a different station, she instantly transposed the conversation into a livelier and more volatile rhythm, and with an inspired inconsequency, a calculated attempt, as it were, to appear scatter-brained, her words flitted brightly round the table, settling here, there and everywhere in the course of their erratic and restless flight.' Despite her great social success there was one specific person whom Maud Cunard could not get on with and that was her daughter Nancy – a member of the Bright Young Things set which so constantly raided the Cavendish and was still dear to the heart of Rosa.

Another vital figure in the lives of the Bright Young Things was another American lady, Laura Corrigan, who, coming from obscure sources, married a multi-millionaire steel man who died six months later, leaving his young widow eighty million dollars in steel shares, which she sold for cash. On arrival in England she rented the home of Edward VII's last mistress, Mrs Keppel, on the understanding that Mrs Keppel's guest list was included as part of the lease. With all these good foundations for social engineering, she arranged to have herself presented at Court by the American Ambassador's wife and then set her hand to the helm of party-giving. At first she was considered completely 'out', but when her social gaucherie became clear she was taken up as another Bright Young Things 'character'. Like Rosa, Laura Corrigan built up her reputation as a 'character' by coming out with all kinds of idiotic remarks and malapropisms. She organized stunt parties for the Bright Young Things and the Cavendish cell of this group involved themselves in such activities as the following, taken from a typical Corrigan shindig:

On the ukelele – Lady Louis Mountbatten
Exhibition dance – Lady Plunket
Tandem Cycle Act – Daphne Vivian, Lord Weymouth, Lady
                         Lettice Lygon and Lord Brecknock.

But their acts were nothing compared with the way Laura Corrigan wound up this particular party. With enormous verve she danced the Charleston in a top hat, then tied a scarf round her skirt to prevent its riding up, and amidst great applause stood on her head. She wore a bright auburn wig, and deliberately contrived to do as many sensational things as she could. All in all she did very well although her motives seem sometimes obscure. She must have realized that she was laughed at but perhaps she also realized that she was admired for her courage, her direct and highly original application to social climbing and her sometimes alarming show-womanship.

Although Laura Corrigan's set of Bright Young Things was almost identical to Rosa Lewis's there is no record that the two women ever met. If they had, however, they would probably have hated each other, for they were so similar. Indeed there could not have been a greater similarity – at least in personality. For although Rosa had to work her way up financially, Laura Corrigan, despite her vast wealth, still had to work her way up the social ladder. They possessed many of the same qualities – courage, independence and prodigious self-determination. But the greatest shared link was that they had both worked to become 'characters' in the synthetic sense. As a result they both spent the rest of their lives living up to being something that they were not – but something that they had become.

Despite the frivolity, the real world of London society that Rosa had known and with which she had been so involved came to an end in the years between 1926 and 1930. Her attitude to this is best typified by the similar attitude of Max Beerbohm, who left London for Rapallo in 1926 in disgust. His view was that London, and in particular, Piccadilly, had been ruined. Gone were the hansom cabs, gas lamps, and the red carpets and the striped awnings outside the great houses during the season. Gone were the great houses – such as Devonshire House – or at least most of them. Other Georgian buildings were being torn down, property speculation was active and the aristocratic landowners of the great town estates were either being forced to sell up or to raise the rents. London was no longer a fit place for an Edwardian gentleman and therefore Beerbohm fled.

The other principal Edwardian in London, however, did not flee. Instead she continued to refuse to accept change, to become even more idiosyncratic, and to retain her own Edwardian world in the Cavendish – a place to which many 'refugees' flocked for nostalgia, for talk of the old days and to relive the old days in the endless flood of champagne that Rosa managed to keep supplying. Admittedly the Bright Young Things amused her, she had her 'family' of Edith and Maud, and she had the escape routes of Jevington and Castle Rock. But despite this there was a mounting ache inside her – a realization that she was no longer part of the actual outside world. Therefore she determined that she would lay seige to time and in the dim, fusty, Edwardian rooms of the

Cavendish she would make her own world – a world of champagne-drugged nostalgia, of the contained gossip of a small community, and of a club where her favourites could do as they liked. But in the end not even Rosa's charisma could prevent the intrusion of the outside world – and now that the twenties were giving way to the thirties, the Bright Young Things began to dim.

Perhaps the best and saddest evidence of Rosa's longing for the past lay in the early morning visits she and the Bright Young Things used to make to Covent Garden market. After a party, a late drinking session at the Cavendish or a night club, she and her protegés would make their way down to the all-night coffee stall in the market. They were usually tight, invariably noisy and no doubt would find the busy, muscular activity in the market 'all too fascinating'. Rosa behaved in just the same exhibitionist way as her young friends.

Yet, years before, when she was building up the Cavendish after the disaster of Excelsior's brief reign, she had been a regular buyer at the market – a working woman who trundled away her purchases on a barrow and was on good, sharp bantering terms with the porters. It is difficult to know what those porters thought of her in the late twenties – an elderly woman dressed in Edwardian clothes accompanied by a group of vacuous young people in evening dress. But one thing is clear – these were not Rosa's best days. In all probability she knew it.

In 1930 Drew, then manager of the Cavendish, retired and was replaced, for a very short time, by the young Dick Brennan. Brennan, now proprietor of the Wig and Pen Club, had been noticed by Rosa on one of her controversial walkabouts at a restaurant. He was then nineteen and a waiter. Throughout the ensuing years he saw her from time to time and they recognized in each other a certain affinity. Brennan had been brought up in the East End and although Rosa had not, she didn't mind people thinking she had been. She passed on to Brennan the inappropriate (but marginally appropriate for him) 'cockney sparrow' persona and it was because of this patronage that when he heard of the Cavendish manager's retirement he phoned Rosa to see if he could get the job. Once he had reminded her that he was her 'cockney sparrow' she gave it to him. It lasted exactly ten days.

To Brennan it was ten days of sheer fantasy during which he hardly ever saw Rosa – and found himself thoroughly resented by the rest of the staff. He was given nothing to do and had no authority. For days he stood around, bewilderedly wondering what on earth to do as he served drinks to the milling Cavendish crowds. Of course, in a sense, there was little to manage, for there were few meals, many IOUs and much drinking. Edith ran the administration and strangers, like Brennan, were resented. So, after his ten days of employment, Brennan returned to the restaurant he had been working in. But he bore no resentment towards Rosa, and indeed is even now one of her most ardent admirers. Brennan, who has developed a certain charisma of his own, perhaps regarded Rosa as a mentor and was therefore blind to her faults. He relates one story with relish. Serving drinks to Rosa's table in a restaurant where he was employed as waiter in his pre-Cavendish days, Brennan asked her party if they would like liqueurs. 'Lick your own,' replied the redoubtable Mrs Lewis, no doubt causing her companions either to laugh uncontrollably – or pray for a thunderbolt. Brennan regards this as a treasured memory – others might feel differently.

Daphne Vivian had married Harry Weymouth, later to be the Marquess of Bath, in 1927 and Rosa and Edith were guests at their wedding at St Martin-in-the-Fields, and afterwards attended the reception, the last one ever given at Dorchester House, just before it was pulled down. In 1930 the Weymouths went to a party at the Cavendish that typified the atmosphere surrounding Rosa at this time. Daphne Vivian writes in her autobiographical book, *Mercury Presides* (published in 1954, under her later name, Daphne Fielding): '. . . we were invited to a party they (Aly Khan and Michael Beary) were giving together at the Cavendish Hotel. . . . The party proved to be an extremely good one. Hutch played the piano, and in the Elinor Glyn room, Rosa Lewis reminisced about everybody's grandparents over champagne.'

Later, in 1933, Daphne Vivian observed:

'Even in those days she was inclined to live in the past. In her rooms, which were lined with photographs of Edwardian bucks and beauties and furnished like an old-fashioned country house, she created a world which she reigned over imperiously . . .

Although many young people have always gone to the Cavendish, more out of curiosity than for any other reason, it is the atmosphere of the Edwardians that has prevailed. . . . Rosa had her favourites, who were often impoverished and she generally managed to wangle it so that their bill was paid by the richer and less favoured ones. One of her pets was a dim little man called Froggy – at least that was the name we knew him by. He seemed to be permanently established at the Cavendish, where he tried to lead a quiet life. Whenever I came to see her, Rosa would say, "Come on, dear, you must come and wake up old Froggy, he's been asking about you." She would then shepherd us all up to his bedroom. Champagne was ordered and the unfortunate Froggy was woken up blinking nervously as the gilded youth (the Bright Young Things) thronged into his room. There was always some sort of Froggy at the Cavendish. . . . Where her favourite young men were concerned, Rosa was like a female tigress protecting her cubs. She sometimes made mistakes. "I won't have that tart coming in here chasing after young So-and-so," she would say as some Leicestershire socialite in full war-paint hove into view. On the other hand, she probably knew exactly who the woman was and only made the mistake on purpose.'

By the end of the year 1930 the rate of unemployment had risen to an unheard-of two and a half million. The world monetary system was breaking down and the payment of war debts, loans to Germany and the growth of profiteering had undermined the stability of the national economy. Financial confidence inside America collapsed, and thousands of small investors found their stocks and shares savings to be completely worthless. Trade with Britain sharply declined and unemployment began to rise alarmingly. Marches of the unemployed to London began from as far afield as Liverpool and Plymouth – marches that demanded new investment, the creation of new industry and that all means tests should be abolished forthwith. In August 1931 a coalition National Government was set up under the leadership of Ramsay Macdonald. This increased taxation, cut salaries of government employees, and cut forces salaries. Another election in November 1931 gave the National Government a mandate and the result was

556 seats for the National Government and 59 seats for the Opposition.

London society took an Edwardian view of the situation and carried on regardless, many deciding that somehow it was the fault of the unemployed that they were unemployed. Others, who were in the deb system, justified themselves by pointing out all the employment they were giving – to caterers, to dressmakers, to florists, to servants and so on. Others just looked at the statistics, looked away from the hunger marchers, avoided thinking about the industrial cities and carried on as before. And although a gradual social conscience *was* stirring in the country, it could not be said that it was stirring at the Cavendish, which was as heavily populated as ever.

In 1932, Aldous Huxley wrote rather dourly of a brief stay at the Cavendish: 'It was like staying in a run-down country house – large comfortable rooms, but everything shabby and a bit dirty. We were not bibulous, so must have been a disappointment to Rosa Lewis. However, she put up with us. Once, I remember, a young man in what the lady novelists call "faultless evening dress" came swaying into our bedroom at almost 2.30 am and had to be pushed out.'

Rosa was *not* anxious to entertain writers in the Cavendish and indeed she had hated and feared them ever since *Vile Bodies* was published in 1930. Sir James Barrie, who often stayed at the Cavendish, was an exception, largely because he had been a friend of Sir William Eden. She had also made a slight exception for the young American journalist who did the profile on her in the *New Yorker*. Rosa gave him a suite of rooms for half the usual price, but invaded his privacy – if you could be said to have privacy at the Cavendish – by arriving unannounced in his bathroom, showing potential clients around his rooms. It was unfortunate that he was in the bath at the time, but predictable that she would deliberately play an embarrassing practical joke on him to make him realize she had teeth. Rosa objected to the article but only because she felt she had to, particularly after the Mary Lawton episode. She knew she was vulnerable, particularly in being such an increasingly idiosyncratic and eccentric public figure. She understood that journalists wanted to probe, to worry at her personality until they discovered what was underneath.

Perhaps she was afraid that they would find out she was not a real person after all. Waugh had merely epitomized a caricature and that was hurtful in itself, for Rosa was fully conscious of what she had become. But she was not fully aware of her true self – that real person who had been overshadowed by the Rosa Lewis cockney sparrow role. What she did realize, however, was that there *was* something to be discovered, something that would have fulfilled her, emotions that demanded love and companionship. And that was not something she cared for a journalist to uncover – or even hint at.

In fact the journalist Joseph Bryan III wrote a perceptive piece on Rosa, and it was published in the *New Yorker* on 16 September 1933. Previous to writing the article, Bryan had received a New Year's card from the Cavendish. There were two photographs on it: one showed a solid and dignified limousine outside an equally solid and dignified hotel; the other showed the courtyard with tables set on scrubbed flagstones, sedate luncheon parties, hovering waiters and the demure proprietress just visible behind an oleander in a tub. A shy terrier was begging from a chair and the card's message read: 'Greetings for 365 Happy Days'. A charming impression of just the kind of hotel you could take Aunt Gwendoline to – and the ironic thing was that you could! But Aunt Gwen definitely would not have been present in Rosa's sanctum where the real fun was to be had.

Bryan recaptures the clientele evocatively in his article, remembering nick-names for her guests.

'The Right Honourable Droopy-Drawers, I later came to learn, was the governor of one of Britain's more important colonies; even so, I suffered several unhappy days before I could watch, without definite queasiness, his practice of stirring butter into his wine. And Lady You-Know-'Oo: was it unreasonable to hope that the foremost woman shot in England (so I was told) would eventually choose another conversational topic than her theory that the Mona Lisa had been painted from a corpse? "'Baffling smile'? Nothing of the sort! Ask any coroner; it's the perfectly familiar *risus sardonicus mortis!*" And Ted: to sit in the same chair, in the same clothes, with the same dead carnation in his lapel, and drink nectarine punch for three solid days –

So, that first stay at Rosa's (you soon drop the "Mrs Lewis"),
I found it easier to leave her other guests to their extraordinary
selves, and most of my time I spent roaming largely through
the hotel.'

He soon penetrated Rosa's holy of holies – her parlour – and his
memories of its are crystal clear. It was not the kind of room,
however, that anyone would be likely to forget easily.

'Most of her souvenirs were in the musty little front room.
Morning whiskeys and luncheon cocktails were served there
(you could stand a spoon in one of the whiskeys), but pre-
eminently it was Rosa's picture gallery. Photographs, paintings,
caricatures of soldiers and children and horses and women and
yachts and dogs completely covered the walls and overflowed
into bulging albums. Two of the pictures are still clear to me.
One was a drawing of a beautiful young man; with apt impu-
dence, he had subscribed it "Mitte sectari Rosa quo locorum
sera moretur," which Horace never meant to be interpreted as
"Forbear to look where Rosa lingers late." '

Avoiding the eccentricities of some of the other guests Bryan
spent a considerable time wandering around, and it is his picture
of the Cavendish which has most accurately preserved its atmosphere of the early thirties.

'There were more pictures in the front hall. A group of
Nelson and his admirals, several superb oils by Henry Alken,
some coaching scenes, and a set of fowling prints, which were
invariably bestowed on every pair of American honeymooners.
"They'll be waitin' when you get 'ome, if I 'ave to wrap 'em
in me best nightie." Pictures, and a highboy, a fireplace with
a big copper jug, two Delft bowls with tulips and hyacinths –
these, and the hall table. It held a Bradshaw, of course, and the
usual dank English blotters, a score of patient letters for
strayed guests, a brass-and-mahogany collection box for
Dr Barnardo's Homes, and sheaves of blue-and-white notepaper, wherefrom the appreciative might learn that the motto
of Mrs Lewis' Cavendish was "In Deo Confido," and its
telegraph address "Excelleth, Piccy."
Straight through the hall was the dining-room, with its

rolling parquet floor, its walls set with vast and peeling mirrors, its queer, carved screen, its French windows opening into the courtyard. And along another hall to your right, and around a corner, and down two steps, was the back parlor, mysteriously known as the Elinor Glyn Room. There was a table, just outside its door, laden with long-empty "cherrybums" of champagne (her idiom for "jeroboams"), each label dated, and crisscrossed with signatures.

You drank only tea in the Elinor Glyn Room, though. It was bright and sunny, with chintz curtains and covers. Rosa's collection of toby jugs and china dogs was kept here, filling the mantlepiece, the cabinets, the taborets. Her guest books of twenty years were in the desk: maharajahs, regimental dinners, film stars, Mayfair. And here hung three more of Rosa's favorite pictures: herself, drawn by Ned Murray, and two drawings of Stefany, which Alfred Munnings and Sir William Orpen once penciled on their tablecloth at dinner. Stefany was the ancient major-domo, deaf and silent. I have heard that he was Emperor Maximilian's bodyguard, that he was a butler of Rothschild's, that he fought under Garibaldi, that he wisely changed his name to Stefany after the Tichborne trial. I have only heard; Stefany said nothing, ever.

And then, of course, there was the upstairs parlor, but you didn't achieve that on your first stay, and some people never achieved it. Not that there was anything remarkable about the upstairs parlor; it had a pair of wide sofas, and some comfortable chairs, and a grand piano. But it was here that Rosa held court.'

'In Deo Confido', or did Rosa really mean 'In Rosa Confido'? Certainly it would have been a more suitable motto for the Cavendish. Many writers must have been inspired by her character and Bryan points out that not only did Evelyn Waugh and Carroll Carstairs get her down on paper but so did Frances Crane in her *The Tennessee Poppy*, in which Rosa became Cissy Pell of the Crown. She also made fictitious appearances in Carl Van Vechten's *Parties* and Emily Hahn's *Congo Solo*. So as Lottie Crump, Mrs Oliver and Cissy Pell, Rosa Lewis sailed as extravagantly through fiction as she sailed through life. Her clients were the same, and Bryan's final memories of Cavendish social life are strange indeed.

'The nights, and the days, and the people. Harry, who was waiting for an estate to be settled; meanwhile, he had only two neckties: an Old Harrovian, and an old Old Harrovian. Johnny, who had just returned from shooting polar bears somewhere off Spitzbergen; he carried his cigarettes in a walrus tooth, and always said "Naydah" for "No." I haven't any idea why. The Danish baroness, who hinted darkly at secret-service work in Martinique, and spoke of Mata Hari as "Poor dear Mata!" The old lady who lay in her darkened room week after week; Rosa sent us up in turn every afternoon to read her the Kai Lung stories. Julian, who could mimic Oxfordese to the infuriation of all Oxonians: "Eh say, Stefany! Eh gless of wat wane fah the gel with the fa'a ha'a." The young professor from the University of Edinburgh who had come down on leave to buy a horse; four days later, horseless, but abominably drunk, he was put on the Flying Scotsman. They had to take off his trousers and shoes to keep him aboard until the train started. And the vicar who said "Curious thing. None of my family ever grows his canine teeth," and said nothing else at all. The vicar, and Lexy, and the Man in the Blues, and Dirty Scott, and Tony, and Rosa again – trotting about the halls, cackling with laughter, shouting at the servants, her amber chain bumping her knees.'

Another incident rather farcically illustrates Rosa's pathological dislike of writers. One of the young men about town who used to haunt the Cavendish in the thirties was a young man named Toby Sloan-Onslow. Onslow had a friend named Hawkins who was rather down on his luck, having lost both his job and his wife in the space of one week. Onslow decided his chum might well be cheered up by a bit of a binge at the Cavendish. For some obscure reason Rosa decided Onslow had introduced a writer on to the premises and strongly took against the unfortunate Hawkins. In the end she refused to admit him and there then began a lunatic battle between Rosa and Onslow – with Onslow intent on smuggling Hawkins in and Rosa equally intent on keeping him out. Rope-ladders and laundry boxes were Onslow's methods, but Rosa confiscated the first and continuously searched the second and the situation became a series of ludicrous and angry confrontations. Eventually Rosa won but Onslow decided to play a trick on her. He called the Cavendish and made a reservation, on behalf of the Portuguese Naval Attaché, for a Commander de Sousa. Onslow then smuggled in Hawkins disguised by a beard, false whiskers and a naval uniform. Rosa received him very politely and for a while the party atmosphere continued. Then, as Hawkins got drunk and began to tell peculiar stories in equally peculiar broken English, Rosa must have seen through the disguise for she called Moon and told him to cancel the 'Commander's' reservation.

It was just this kind of game that Rosa Lewis loved. She thoroughly enjoyed the matriarchal role she played to the younger set in the Cavendish. Confiscation, searching, gating and meta-phorically slapped wrists were the punishments she applied to her 'naughty' boys and girls – it was as if she were the forbidding but kind matron in a mixed and rather more than permissive prep school. She really should have had a nickname (Droopy-Drawers?) and all would have been complete.

Painters were not as disliked as writers, presumably because no one had come up with a caricature of her. Sir Alfred Munnings was a Cavendish customer and of course in the past both Sickert and Whistler had been associates of the bellicose Eden. Augustus John came to the Cavendish in the thirties, usually with his lover Sylvia Gough, in whose divorce case he later featured as one of several co-respondents. John, of course, was also a friend of Margot Asquith (Ribblesdale's sister-in-law). He didn't paint Rosa but others did. An American painter, Murray, did an excellent charcoal sketch of her in the style of Sargent. The most famous, however, was a real abomination and was painted by Guevara in the mid-twenties and exhibited at the Royal Academy. It depicted Rosa reclining on a sofa, her skirt catching the firelight and 'her expressive face turned tensely towards the painter' as a contemporary newspaper account put it.

Few meals were served in the Cavendish during the thirties. There were snacks to accompany the booze and overnight guests were served with breakfast – if any of them could face it after the night before. The American association continued and a large number of guests were often of that nationality. Amongst the most notable party-givers was Jimmy Walker, Mayor of New York, who had come across to see London's Chief Magistrate on an official visit and who successfully eased himself out of all the pomposity at an all-night Cavendish party.

But it would be wrong to give the impression that Rosa in the thirties was always a decadent matriarch. With some people she found she could relax, be herself – and give. One client, a Mrs Corbett remembered:

'I took my daughter (aged about four) to visit her at the hotel. She was delighted to see Barbara, but was apparently very anxious to talk to me privately so Barbara was put in charge of the head-waiter. When I next saw my daughter she was sitting on the counter of the "Dispense" being stood glasses of milk and chocolate by most of the downstairs staff. Mrs Lewis then insisted that we should both go with her and spend the day at her house in Sussex. After all that milk-and-chocolate, it was not very surprising that, after we had gone some way, Barbara announced that she felt sick. I asked Mrs Lewis if we could stop for a few moments, but she said No, and from somewhere produced a large dress box, handed it to the child saying, "There you are, darling – be sick in that. Be sick anywhere you like." I think the size of the receptacle so staggered my daughter that she managed to control the sickness! Perhaps Mrs Lewis knew more about children that I thought.

We had a lovely day, and I thought Mrs Lewis seemed to be so happy to be there, and she showed us all round the house and garden. I got the impression that she liked being in that house more than she liked being at Cowes. Maybe that she rarely, I believe, had any visitors there, or only the ones she was fond of, so that it was a complete rest and change for her. I felt very pleased and honoured at being asked to spend the day there.'

This was typical of Rosa's pleasure in genuine, ordinary people, despite the fact that she really couldn't stand the company of young children.

By 1933 the depression was slowly lifting. Rosa was now sixty-six. Unemployment, however, was still at the devastating peak of just under three million but fell by half-a million as the year progressed. Industrial production began to recover, suburban development to appear and 'modern' furniture and ornaments to be produced. A social conscience was beginning to develop in some sections of society and the Oxford Union Debating Society caused a stink by passing the motion 'This House would in no circumstances fight for king and country' by 275 votes to 153. Books from the later twenties such as Sassoon's *Memoirs of an Infantry Officer* and Graves's *Goodbye to All That* had created an anti-war mood, and the Cavendish became a stormy battleground between the young anti-war lobby and the older, near apoplectic officers of the First World War. Even some naughty public school chaps at Wellington, notably Churchill's nephews, Giles and Esmond Romilly, said no to the Officers' Training Corps. They became even naughtier when they published a left-wing magazine for public schools named *Out of Bounds*. Its edict was 'to champion the forces of progress against the forces of reaction on every front, from compulsory military training to propagandist teaching'. Meanwhile no one paid much attention to the sinister fascist rumblings in Europe, Unity Mitford was drinking coffee with Hitler in Germany, and Mosley was parading his Blackshirts.

But despite the gathering social conscience, the society gossip columnist was in his heyday – and of course the greatest of them all was Lord Castlerosse. However, it was his lady friend and later wife, Doris Delavigne, that Rosa singularly disliked, although no doubt the feeling was mutual. Rosa summed up her opinion of the lady by saying, 'Young Doris may go far on those legs of hers, but mark my words she doesn't know how to make a man comfortable'. She was dead right there. But before examining the rather grisly personality of Doris, it is important to take a look at her unfortunate husband.

Lord Beaverbrook was merely being his usual astute self when he hired Viscount Castlerosse to write a weekly society gossip column in the *Sunday Express*. At the same time Beaverbrook was running his great attempt at morale boosting during the depression – the Empire Crusade. But this was not necessarily a circulation raiser and Castlerosse was. His column was witty and indiscreet without being malicious and none of its subjects thought of themselves as victims. In fact they were probably competing desperately to get in it. Being a real-life aristocrat,

Castlerosse simply wrote about his own friends and acquaintances. As he was eccentric, bibulous and a gourmand he had plenty of opportunity to meet them and observe their private lives. He also had an enormous personality, an enormous body and a violent temperament. And it was this temperament that was considerably inflamed by his marriage to Doris Delavigne.

Doris was born in 1900 in Streatham with a background of old Belgian nobility. She grew up to be blonde, beautiful and artistically talented. She was also shrewd. At first she worked in the rag trade and then bought a hairdressing business called Louis in the Champs-Elysées in Paris. Doris made a great impact on London society, largely because of her vastly expensive tastes. Castlerosse, despite his work for Beaverbrook, was impoverished and lived on credit, yet found his marriage to Doris inescapable. He was obsessed and very jealous of her association with other men. Oddly enough she was also jealous of *his* activities. They both had the same violent temperament and advertised the gossip column well by having scenes in public which were always noisy and sometimes resulted in physical violence. No doubt Beaverbrook was delighted by the living farce of the Castlerosse marriage as it was obviously a circulation booster. But apart from the pain this brought to the two people involved, it was also pretty disgusting to run, on one hand, the Empire Crusade to boost the morale of the unemployed, and on the other hand to print Castlerosse's column, which exclusively described the activities of the rich and the favoured.

Daphne Vivian was a personal friend of Doris as well as Rosa, and for this reason she was determined to make them friends. Needless to say her efforts were doomed from the very beginning. She set up a meeting over drinks between Rosa and Doris at the Cavendish but the atmosphere was icy with mutual antipathy. Amongst other social remarks that Rosa made to Doris, remembered by Daphne Vivian, was 'You should write a book and call it "Round the World in Eighty Beds".' Without doubt, this was one relationship which had very little future.

In this same year of 1933, Nazi power had arrived with the burning of the Reichstag and the constitution in Germany had been set aside by Hitler. World peace now depended on Hitler and Mussolini. But despite the fact that by 1934 Mosley's British

Union of Fascists had a membership of approximately twenty thousand, already causing considerable disturbances in Jewish areas, post-depression Britain was in a mood of relief rather than gloom. Also, amidst the higher echelons of society there were certain pro-German sympathies which were carefully fostered by Ribbentrop, the German ambassador. One of the strongest of these sympathizers was Unity Mitford, sister of Nancy, one of the Cavendish's Bright Young Things. As a deb Unity had been an unmitigated disaster and, as a person, was leading a purposeless life. Then, at her sister Diana's house, she met Mosley and suddenly her life had the purpose it was lacking. The bedroom she shared with her younger sister Jessica at Swinburne, the Mitford country-house, was soon covered with Nazi insignia and Unity was already the proud owner of a black shirt. Jessica, a keen Communist, hit back by covering her side with her own party's insignia. Later Unity was to meet Hitler in Germany, and later still the Mitford parents were to be fêted there.

There was no direct Nazi influence in the Cavendish, however, despite the pro-German leanings of some of the Bright Young Things, and Hutch played on in the dusty Edwardian lounges whilst Rosa held court in her parlour, or sometimes in the Elinor Glyn room. In 1934 a royal marriage further cushioned the public from the sinister events in Europe. Cavendish parties and glowing obsequious newspaper supplements celebrated the marriage of Prince George (later the Duke of Kent) to Princess Marina of Greece. In 1935 there was even more cause for escapist ceremony with King George v's Jubilee.

The Government realized that they could use this occasion very much to their advantage. The time was obviously ripe for an election and the Jubilee could be used as excellent propaganda. The celebration would ostensibly mark the end of the Depression and therefore they should re-create all the pomp and circumstance of Queen Victoria's Golden Jubilee. Fireworks, street parties, village green dancing, a state drive through London, a thanksgiving service at St Paul's – everything went off well and there was a mood of national rejoicing. Two months later, carefully based on the synthetically created national mood, the election took place. As a result the Conservatives, with the addition of National Liberal and National Labour members, had an over-all majority of almost 250 seats. Ramsay MacDonald, his Labour reputation discredited as a result of his association with an almost totally Conservative government, was defeated at Seaham and crept in the back door of the House of Commons, as a member for the Scottish Universities. He was replaced as Prime Minister by Stanley Baldwin.

Rosa Lewis gave a ball at Castle Rock in celebration of the Jubilee and then, anxious to join the all-night celebrations at the Cavendish, flew back to London – a form of transport that she had not used before. Then, little more than a fortnight later, the Cavendish was hit by a major scandal, which made Rosa both furious and wary. Furious with herself for being indiscreet and wary that such a situation should ever happen again. As the scandal dragged in Buckingham Palace, she must have been doubly aware that in the days of Edward as Prince of Wales, when she was in her prime, such a situation could never have happened. She had been employed for her discretion – and married for her discretion. Now, in her old age, she had failed to be discreet. It was very galling.

Buckingham Palace had, over and around the period of the Jubilee, become the hub of fashionable society. Many of this élite chose to come to the Cavendish on the night of 14 May 1935 to celebrate Lord Revelstoke's victory in a breach of promise case. Revelstoke was a regular at the Cavendish, a favourite of Rosa's and therefore the champagne was uncorked in no uncertain manner. On 16 May the story of the night's activities appeared on the front page of the *Express*, scooped by an initiative-taking reporter named Henry McNally. Discovering that an interesting party had taken place, especially at the Cavendish, which meant *more* than interesting, he phoned a titled lady known to be a likely guest and assured her that he was a member of the Cavendish hotel staff. McNally then asked her if she had left a diamond necklace behind in the hotel, to which the lady replied in the negative. He then rang off, leaving her presumably to nurse her hangover, and strolled down to the Cavendish. Posing as a drinker (and definitely not revealing himself as a reporter!) he got Rosa going on the subject of the Revelstoke revelry. She gave him all he needed and the rest was a cinch. McNally's story read as follows:

HIGH JINKS IN JERMYN-STREET

Celebrating the Revelstoke Verdict

Daily Express Special Representative

'Diamonds, rubies and pearls sparkled and glistened at London's strangest party until long after dawn yesterday.

Scarlet, gold and silver were the uniforms the men wore as they celebrated the legal victory of Lord Revelstoke in the breach of promise case.

The party was "thrown" in the so-called cocktail bar where Lord Revelstoke met Angela Joyce. Actually it is a sort of private sitting-room in a Jermyn-Street hotel.

ALL FOR A BET

"It was all for a bet," the owner of the hotel said. "I bet I would throw a party if Revelstoke won. There were about a hundred people present, most of whom had come direct from Buckingham Palace. The men were in uniform, with full decorations. Look at that busby there on the table. Someone left it behind.

They drank eighteen magnums of champagne and other drinks. We took down the photograph of Revelstoke from the wall and toasted it. The whole party did not cost me more than £48, but if it had cost £100 it could not have been better.

I had only three servants on duty; no flunkeys, you know. So there'll be nothing in the newspapers about the party. If you've got flunkeys, they always ring up the newspapers and sell the story."

I looked around the room. It was so different from the cocktail-bars further along the street. There was no chromium plating, no futuristic furniture. There was nothing of 1935. It was the world of 1910. Faded old paintings and coloured engravings of "The Cries of London" decorated the walls. It might have been a hundred miles from London. Here was none of the shrill laughter, none of the chatter of "White Ladies" and "Sidecars" that seemed to be all the conversation of the other bars outside.

A white Aberdeen terrier and a white Pekinese slept on the hearthrug.

MARCONIGRAM

A Marconigram was delivered. "I wonder if I have made a thousand," the old lady said as she read it, "or lost a couple. I don't mind being done with my eyes open. If I'm a mug I deserve to lose."

"But," she went on, "it was a wonderful party. I'm sure Lord and Lady Revelstoke were ever so happy. It was such an ordeal for them. But he was a *man* to fight the case!"

On my right was a table loaded with champagne glasses, and with them a bearskin.

"You see," she said, "the men were all in uniform and the women blazed with diamonds and rubies. You never saw such pearls! They came straight from the Palace. And the papers will never hear about it. He left his busby behind . . ." '

The next day another story concerning the controversial party appeared in the *Express*. It read:

THE OLD SCHOOL ARE SHOCKED

From Palace to Cocktail Party

'Many of the "old school" were horrified yesterday by the disclosure that guests had gone direct from Buckingham Palace to join festivities at cocktail bars and other places wearing uniforms and decorations. It is an unwritten law of the Army that an officer or ex-officer should not appear in a public place in uniform, except on duty. . . . '

The fact that it was not the 'done thing' to appear socially in full regalia was not the full story. The Cavendish still had its reputation for being a high-class knocking shop and such a distinguished company's celebrating such a victory in such circumstances was definitely regarded as highly dangerous to a large number of reputations. Rosa fully realized this, and also realized that not only had she been indiscreet but she had made a complete fool of herself by talking, albeit unknowingly, to that breed she was reputed to be able to sniff out a hundred miles away – the hated writer/journalist. But above all, what was even more depressing, Rosa must have realized that she was old.

This, of course, was not the only time during this period that

Rosa and the Cavendish appeared in the press, although usually there were fewer ramifications. One newspaper reported a case where Rosa appeared as a witness for the prosecution against an assistant housekeeper who had been employed at the Cavendish. It read:

DOG FINDS WOMAN CROUCHING IN CORNER OF HOTEL

' "The more I shook her the more things fell out," declared Rosa Lewis of the Cavendish Hotel, Jermyn Street, giving evidence today. The woman, charged with stealing silk stockings, bottles of stout, port and other articles, was Marie Turner who had been an assistant housekeeper in the hotel.

"She had taken things from every room she had been in," said the proprietress. "The dog showed me where she was crouching in a dark corner of the passage: she was trying to get out of a side door." '

Apart from this, litigation was confined to Rosa's seizing luggage or personal possessions when those out of her favour refused to pay their bill. On one occasion she took to court an American family who refused to pay up on the grounds that the Cavendish was too noisy at night for them to sleep. She won her case against the family although what the judge did not realize was that one of Rosa's principal witnesses to the Cavendish's being an oasis of night-time peace was deaf!

In fact there were many instances when Rosa could have been prosecuted herself, for she consistently served drinks out of hours. She was only once prosecuted for this – which was fairly miraculous. Colonel Hargreaves, a regular at the Cavendish in the late thirties, pointed out that Rosa had a certain system about out-of-hours drinking. She would try to keep it legal by dragging in a resident who could then play 'host' to his 'guests' with Rosa adjusting his bill to comply with normal round-buying. If no resident would agree to this (and they would be considerably out of favour if they didn't) then she would merely serve the drinks and take a risk. Hargreaves added wearily that he was often called out of bed by Rosa at more or less any hour of the night to 'host' her parties.

One interesting and thoughtful eyewitness to Rosa's personality in the late thirties was Jan Meekins, who often went to

the Cavendish with a group of racing drivers from the old
Brooklands track at Weybridge in Surrey. Rosa advised Jan to
'make the best of herself' and to exploit men for all she was
worth. She remembers one phrase that Rosa used, 'Life is like a
rainbow. You grasp your happiness'. Jan Meekins went on to say
that Rosa only liked or respected attractive women, that she was a
snob, a materialist, a cynic and was very money-conscious. Yet
she liked her, particularly for what Mrs Meekins called 'her
cockney wit'. As a shy person she felt safe with Rosa, and as a
beauty of her time was no doubt singled out for patronage. A
painter, Jan Meekins had a particular eye for the beauty that Rosa
was still meant to possess. 'Beauty', says Mrs Meekins 'was differently classified in the thirties. Pure beauty was meant to be the
first "flush of youth", i.e. at about seventeen or eighteen. Perhaps
she had this. Beyond that – if you were beautiful – you were
termed a "fine looking woman." Rosa was not this. In terms of
classical painting she had a "peasant" type face.' Jan Meekins
went on to add that she felt Rosa sometimes resented the third
generation of young, wealthy people, who were beyond her in
thought and fashion. Perhaps she felt they had not won their
spurs if their grandfathers were not true Edwardians and their
fathers, if they had survived, were not veterans of the First
World War.

Robin McDouall knew Rosa from 1926 until the time of her
death. Now Secretary of the Carlton Club, he remembers her as a
'woman who never let him down' – or very rarely let him down!
Part of the young Cavendish set, he used to go to the Cavendish
for the parties which were tremendous fun, with Daphne (now
Fielding) and Harry Weymouth (later the Marquess and Marchioness of Bath):

'They were the most scintillating and most handsome of all
the couples there. I had a high old time but dreaded Rosa
meeting my mother who once came to the Cavendish to see
friends. I definitely thought she'd split on me. But she didn't.
Instead she offered my mother champagne which she refused.
Undismayed Rosa gave her soup and sat on a sofa with her,
the very essence of good taste and respectability. She was only
to embarrass me once and that was when I took the wife of an

American film director for a late drink at the Cavendish one night. I had absolutely no designs on her but Rosa, thinking I had, shouted out that a room had been reserved for me. It was an awkward moment.'

This was typical of Rosa's service industry for her Bright Young Things – reassuring mothers and smoothing the way for assignations was instinctive and she did it automatically, even if she did slip up from time to time! McDouall continued by saying, 'There were always two kinds of groups in the Cavendish – the raffish set and the respectable set'. Somehow they seemed to co-exist quite happily yet separately, the one seemingly unaware of the other's existence. The presence of clergymen, dowagers and non-decadent colonels helped Rosa to reassure even the most troubled of mothers.

The cloistered world of the Cavendish continued until the Second World War, when, as in the first, it took on a new lease of life. Like a battered, sightless galleon the Cavendish sailed blindly through the events that charted the pre-war period. The death of George v at Sandringham in 1936, the new King's friendship with Mrs Wallis Simpson and his eventual abdication, the Spanish Civil War, the Coronation of George vi, and the more immediate events leading to the Second World War were all obviously reflected in the Cavendish's clientele, but not in its proprietor, who had years ago given up all pretence of living in the modern world. The Bright Young Things were growing older now and no longer required her matriarchal involvement. Rosa reminisced, indulged in nostalgia, and lived in the past. Then suddenly with the outbreak of the Second World War in 1939 she awoke – and once more became fully involved in the present. She was needed again – and despite the fact that Rosa Lewis was now seventy-two she was more than ready to respond.

SEVEN

The Past Becomes the Present

1939–52

'People only come to the Cavendish to bounce cheques and pee.'
ROSA LEWIS

ON 3 SEPTEMBER 1939, THE OUTBREAK OF THE SECOND WORLD war was announced on the radio at 11 am by Neville Chamberlain. He was preceded by a selection from *Princess Ida*, Parry Jones singing 'The Passionate Shepherd', and a recorded talk entitled 'Making the Most of Tinned Foods'. Eight minutes later, sirens began to sound over Greater London and shortly afterwards over other parts of the country. In the Cavendish, Rosa half slept through the King's broadcast at 6 pm that evening. He said: 'In this grave hour, perhaps the most fateful in our history, I send to every household of my peoples, both at home and overseas, this message . . . For the sake of all that we ourselves hold dear and of the world's order and peace, it is unthinkable that we should refuse to meet the challenge . . . To this high purpose, I now call my people at home and my peoples across the seas. I ask them to stand firm and united in this time of trial.'

The weather that day matched the mood of the country. The sky was dark with a slow falling drizzle and the interior of the Cavendish was dim and ethereal. That night there was the first radio instalment of J. B. Priestley's *Let the People Sing*, and the rest of the evening's broadcasting included a service, some records and Sandy Macpherson at the theatre organ. There was a more escapist feeling in Rosa's front parlour and soon the champagne was clouding the first war nerves of the Cavendish set.

A few hours after the outbreak of war Parliament rushed through the National Service (Armed Forces) Act which specified that all men between eighteen and forty-one, providing they were fit, were liable for military service. In 1941 a further Act made women liable for call-up and the age limit for men was extended from forty-one to fifty-one. By the end of 1939, 727,000 men were registered, in 1940, 4,100,000 and in 1941, 2,222,000. Those coming to the Cavendish, were, as in the First World War, officers only, and other ranks would not get a look in – even if they could afford it, which they couldn't. The wives of the lower ranks of the services were very poverty-stricken. Right up until 1944, for instance, the wife of a private soldier with two small children received twenty-five shillings a week, plus seven shillings stopped from her husband's pay. This meant that he was being paid the princely sum of one shilling a day for leaving home and putting his life at immediate risk. It was not until 1944 that this income was raised to sixty shillings a week – which was still barely adequate.

Although considerably less physically barbaric than the First World War, the Second World War still took a dreadful toll of lives. Of 5,900,000 men and women serving in the war, 265,000 were killed, 277,000 were wounded and 172,000 were captured. This is far greater than the civilian death toll which amounted to 61,000 dead and 86,000 badly injured out of a population of 40,000,000.

Suddenly there were military uniforms everywhere and once again the Cavendish buzzed with the clatter of urgent, new life: early comings and goings, gas masks, confusion over air-raid shelters, a sudden revival of good food in the restaurant (salmon and game birds from Rosa's country clients), and Rosa, the vinegary old matriarch, presiding sometimes geriatrically and sometimes with abrasive sharpness over her élitist bolt-hole.

Rosa's dislike of change had been further catalysed in the years before the outbreak of war by the continuing demolition of Edwardian London. Many of the great houses where she and her team had cooked were now heaps of rubble. Much of the east side of Berkeley Square had been torn down in 1937 and the Adelphi, Chesterfield House and Lansdowne House had also gone. With them gone, her old way of life was no longer in evidence. As she dozed on her Cavendish throne, Rosa remembered the days when she had been an important figure in the lives of so many distinguished men and women. Their paeans of praise echoed down the decades. 'My dear Mrs Lewis – words cannot express – a magnificent meal – your wonderful cooking – your beautiful girls – your great efficiency – how do you do it – my dear Mrs Lewis.' But they had dropped her now, dropped her years ago when 'Kingy' died. She had been useful, and now she was useless.

Except for the war – and the faint return of her beloved 'boys'. But they had not really returned, she knew that. They were all dead, years before in the Flanders mud. They were dust now, just like the environs of her former, culinary glory. The King (the *only* King to her), Eden, Ribblesdale, her 'boys' and the great houses. All dead. All dust.

The new architectural style of the times was ill-defined, with abstract designs, Constance Spry flower arrangements, tubular steel and glass furniture, black glass pilasters, Lalique ornaments and wall lights – and so on. Very *à la mode*. Very uncertain.

The outbreak of war saw the Cavendish in a run-down state and during the war its reception rooms had the atmosphere of a clubby mess-room, while the bedrooms were used to accommodate as many people as possible. There was no room service or at least if there was it was very erratic, and good food was for residents only, with a good deal of booze which obviously came from the still well-stocked cellar. The shadows of her 'boys', these World War II officers, were so different. They seemed older, more sophisticated, less vulnerable. Nevertheless Rosa rallied to their needs, although she was not as good at finding good, clean tarts for them as she had been. In fact she must have been growing very senile for complaints began to be received from Fortnum's about Mrs Lewis's behaviour outside their staff entrance (which part of the Cavendish faced). Apparently she had been in the habit of accosting the girls as they left after a day's work in the shop and asking if they'd 'like a little drink dear' with the officers in the Cavendish. They did not appreciate the invitation.

The five war years were a tapestry of comfort and adrenalin, courage and disaster as far as Rosa and the Cavendish were concerned. Two typical reminiscences set the scene of that period. The first comes from George Barrett:

'One felt honoured to be invited by Rosa to join her in the front room of the Cavendish. I was a junior army officer who spent many of my leaves from my regiment, the Royal Ulster Rifles, at the Cavendish. Vast quantities of champagne were consumed nightly but I was never asked to pay. Rosa would weigh up who, among the assembled guests, was in the best position (more often than not an American General) to pay or share the total bill and this they would do with little or no hesitation. Among Rosa's regulars I recall Prince Paul (later King) of Greece who also was never asked to pay for drinks – he never seemed to have any money anyway.'

Secondly, McDonough Russell remembers how he met Rosa for the first time a few days before the Dieppe landing:

'I'd been summoned for an interview at the Air Ministry at some ungodly hour such as 9.00 am on a Sunday morning from my station at Hereford. My club was full and my taxi-cab driver said that every hotel I mentioned was full. Asked for advice he could think only of the Ritz 'or one of those bed and breakfast places in Bayswater – and we could spend half the night trying to find one with a bed.' As an afterthought he added 'Of course the old Cavendish is only round the corner. They tell me it's never half full.' So we went there.'

When he arrived Russell was given a room on the first floor by Edith and told 'there'd be no dinner owing to "difficulties".' He was also told that he should see 'Madam', who would 'never forgive her for letting an officer go without sharing a drink'.

He went down to Rosa's parlour where he was greeted by, 'Have a glass of wine, dear boy. Is your photograph here? You really must bring one next time. I have photographs of all my officers.' Russell was handed a glass of good champagne and soon saw that he was in distinguished company. Also in the room was Sir John Squire, poet, parodist and editor of the *London Mercury*. He was with fighter-pilot Richard Hillary. Alex Waugh was there too and McDonough Russell has a vague recollection of Rosa's introducing him as 'the nice brother of that rude writer'.

Despite the fact that he had asked for a call at seven, no one came, his shoes were unbrushed, and the water in the marble basin was cold. He could find no one downstairs to pay, and eventually managed to unlock the front door after a furious struggle with a battery of bolts and chains. Next time he was in London Russell dutifully returned to the Cavendish, saw Edith and explained the problem. She refused, however, to give him a bill. Later he paid his respects to Rosa and remembers that she 'blinked at me and said, "Did you bring the photograph? Don't

forget next time. Have a glass of wine!" J. C. Squire was there
again. I'd have liked to drag him out to dinner somewhere but
just in time realized that he was really very drunk indeed. He told
me Richard Hillary had been killed.'

Russell's anecdote particularly well summarizes Rosa's spirited
and still commanding decline.

Yet another example of Rosa's perpetual, quixotic generosity
comes from another ex-officer:

> 'At the outbreak of war I enlisted in the Coldstream and
> spent its first period at the Guards' Depot, Caterham, and the
> Training Battalion, Pirbright, whence I went to London for
> dinner when possible. On one occasion I was broke and asked
> Rosa if I could sign my bill, as I had done before. Instead of
> just saying yes, she asked me into her office for a glass of
> champagne and questioned me about the material effect of
> enlisting.
>
> When my bill arrived for signature it had with it an evelope
> containing ten fivers – "the end of the war will do, dear". I
> repaid this on my way to OCTU in 1940 and didn't see Rosa
> again.'

Daphne Fielding also recalls, in her biography *Mercury Presides*,
something of the atmosphere of those war years: 'On my rare
visits to London I usually stayed at the Cavendish, where Rosa
welcomed her favourites back on leave as she had done in the war
before this one . . . Whenever I heard a siren I felt an increasing
need for company and a drink to give me courage; and since both
were available at the Cavendish, there was little need to move out
of the hotel. Rosa was so generous to all of us that we wondered
how she ever managed to make the hotel pay.'

Another war-time refugee in the Cavendish was de Vere Cole's
ex-wife, Mavis, now married to Sir Mortimer Wheeler and
sowing a large number of wild oats. She found the hotel an ideal
base and her biographer, Roderic Owen, in *Beloved and Beautiful*,
wrote:

> 'The Cavendish – when fit and ready to resume her usual
> practice of juggling several balls in the air at a time, Mavis
> found the Cavendish ideal. And so it was, for anyone favoured

by its proprietress, ex-cook to royalty, Rosa Lewis. Blitzed in 1943, the hotel survived as a country-house extension into the heart of the West End, replete with grand but battered furniture and multitudinous pictures. The Cavendish had such chic; it was *the* place, in a Café Royal or Tour Eiffel sense. Back to the Cavendish came those who'd been to the Gargoyle, the Boeuf sur le Toit, the Suivi and the Nuthouse. Herself a cracking snob, Rosa Lewis would have known a lot about Horace de Vere Cole; and that would have conferred a 'suitable' background on Mavis, making her excesses (when she brought a man back or met a man there) "all right". Rosa had *entrain*; she created a chummy atmosphere and the guests were introduced to each other as if at a party. Champagne flowed. Someone paid – Rosa decided whose turn; her calculation a shrewd asessment of willingness and capability.'

Mavis de Vere Cole, 'beloved and beautiful', was a tragic figure and later, with her shooting of Daphne Fielding's brother, Lord Vivian, the attendant sensational court case, her ghosted articles in the *Empire News*, her spell in Holloway Prison and her lonely death, was to be a typical casualty of the Cavendish style of living. One of Mavis's seducers of the war-time period was a young Canadian naval officer who was ten years younger (she was by then thirty-five). After an idyllic time at the Cavendish he had a pang of guilt and wrote to her saying: 'Every time I've thought of you not staying at the Cavendish today I've thanked the Lord. Believe it or not, I have always gone there as a single man and I had never realized before what a lecherous establishment it is. I'm really very sorry I persuaded you to come there although to me *our* stay was heaven.' One can almost hear, if only the word had been in common usage at that time, both Rosa and Mavis loudly chorusing 'Bullshit!' That the Cavendish was a lecherous establishment could not be denied but certainly the young officer's tone was more than hypocritical.

Despite the warning Mavis de Vere Cole was still haunting the Cavendish in 1944, this time deeply in love with one of Rosa's American 'boys' – Stewart Bryan, an already married US Air Force Major. She wrote in her diary on 15 October 1944 about her first meeting with him: 'Had a delicious bath and took myself off to see Rosa and Edith. Very few people there but one or two acquaintances . . . Met charming American called Stewart Bryan. Unlike most Americans he was dignified and very *comme il faut.*' On the next day, 16 October, she wrote: 'Had tea with Edith. She so pleased! Stewart asked me about theatres. Was invited to a party at Mirabelle, didn't go, but joined in drinking champagne with some chaps and their girls who were celebrating safe return. Went home and cooked some ham and eggs. Felt very tired but restless. S. telephoned and later called. Had long talk about books – thought he would never go, but he did 2.30 am.'

Years later, on 26 September 1964, Mavis de Vere Cole wrote to Stewart Bryan about their meetings at the Cavendish. Time was running out for Bryan, however, and he was soon to die of a liver disease. 'My diary of 20 years ago – the only one I have ever kept – is always close at hand to tell me of the rainy, dreary afternoon at Rosa's when God said 'Let there be light'; The rather mixed up evening that followed in the blue chair by the gas log and then the appalling taxi ride back to Jermyn Street – a fitful night and then . . . I was admitted to where there was and for me ever since has been light, warmth and love that passeth my understanding but not my yearning for its continuance as long as I live.'

Mavis de Vere Cole died alone in 1969 of drink and drugs. In a way Mavis and Rosa had similar personalities. One aspect of Mavis's was well summed up by her second husband, Sir Mortimer Wheeler. He said 'When she imagined a thing it became actual and real to her. It wasn't that she was telling a lie, it was the truth misplaced.' Exactly the same description could apply to Rosa Lewis.

By this time Rosa had sold her house at Jevington and also had sold Castle Rock – to the hated Royal Yacht Squadron, who could at last offer their ladies a sizeable retreat. In fact Rosa had originally tried to sell the house to Maud Puckering, Edith Jeffreys' sister, but she refused, pointing out how expensive the place would be to keep up, as well as the problems of the escalating rates.

Throughout the war Rosa and Edith's main male support was Charles Ingram who, like other members of the staff before him, had become an all-round helpmate. Besides Ingram and a few part-timers there was the still indestructible Moon, looking more and more like an elderly prawn with perpetual ill-grace. He would grumblingly open the front door late at night, ushering the guests into the Cavendish hallway as if ushering them into a dank family vault. In the morning he equally unwillingly went to fetch taxis, obeying the instructions of Rosa and Edith with grim apathy. Finally there was Mrs Urquhart who was both cook and housekeeper and very much the opposite of the more eccentric and dilapidated of Rosa's staff. She was a fresh, neat Scotswoman and had the air of the perfect confidential servant.

One of the most perceptive visitors to the Cavendish was the biographer Molly Izzard, wife of Ralph Izzard, ex-foreign correspondent of the *Daily Mail*. They both regularly stayed at the Cavendish when on leave and remembered it with affection. Although they never knew exactly what the bill was going to be, the Izzards found the Cavendish a rather different kind of bolt-hole from the majority of Rosa's clients. Separated for so many months of the year, they wanted to lead private lives in a public place – and the Cavendish was the only place where they could do this. They were given a room (or sometimes rooms) where a fire burnt snugly in the grate and food, wine and champagne were served. There was pheasant and salmon from the country, the table-linen was still spotless and there was a profusion of flowers. In contrast, the once elegant courtyard was unkempt and covered with a thick layer of soot. Ribblesdale's furniture littered the hallway and reception rooms, as did his prints and engravings. A huge coal fire roared in the grate of the hall and next to it sat Rosa. Molly Izzard remembers her as often asleep or nodding, but still very much aware of what was going on. For if someone she disapproved of hurried past her, she would come to, and in a rasping, harsh growl she would give vent to some obscenity about their appearance, the state of their underclothes or the state of their sex-lives.

Many of the rooms in the Cavendish were shuttered and Edith scurried around those that were open, managing Rosa and reprimanding the customers if they gave her too much to drink. She was not to get 'over-excited'. It is clear now that Rosa was renouncing her role of universal mother, and Edith was playing a similar but more restricted maternal part – mothering Rosa exclusively. She could 'manage her', could 'keep her calm' and could prevent her from becoming 'over-excited'.

Rosa always referred to Ralph Izzard as young 'Legard', confusing him with a young cricketer she had known in her Edwardian glory. She often used to confuse people now with those silvan ghosts from the past and people began to realize which Rosa-bestowed name was relevant to which individual. Molly Izzard was not an intimate of Rosa's, but few people were at this time. But she recognized her as an arch-snob, an embittered servant, obsessed with her own problems. In Mrs Izzard's view the Cavendish was an adult extension of the nursery, presided over by Rosa as Nanny. Timid children would treat her with great care lest her tongue should molest them. More robust children were allowed to treat her with greater familiarity. However they could only go so far, and they knew it. There was even nursery food, scrambled egg and often bread-and-butter pudding. The hotel was now Mrs Lewis's private residence and her guests were 'invited' to it. Spoiled, capricious, she treated her own servants (with the exception of Edith) in a feudal manner but retained many of them long after their usefulness was over. She was aware that a good number of them could never survive in a conventional hotel and she was equally aware that some of them had nowhere they could go to retire.

'A disreputable version of Brown's' was how Mrs Izzard classified the current aura of the hotel. 'A naughty nursery' where no questions were asked and at a time when no self-consciousness was present. She was sure however that Rosa despised many of her clients and deliberately acted badly on whim. Yet Rosa not only catered for the domestic welfare of her guests, she catered for their very life-styles. So many of her clients were insecure, rich, publicity-hungry people, and they gathered around her fading jam-pot, knowing that she would serve them – and their needs – well. That was one service she could still offer, even if her remaining energies were fast disappearing.

Despite the fact that Rosa tended to confuse the two wars, and many of the personalities involved, she still held court to a glittering array of World War II heroes, both English and American. Amongst them were Lord Lovat (Ribblesdale's grandson) who led the commando raid on Dieppe, Richard

Hillary, Patrick Leigh Fermor, who kidnapped a German general in Crete, John Alsop who parachuted into France, Colonel Wakely of the Rhine, and so on.

In September 1940 serious bombing began on London. In May 1941 the Cavendish was hit. A land-mine blew out the front whilst incendiaries destroyed the top storey. The first bomb that hit the Cavendish killed one of the hotel's last remaining eccentrics. The second demolished one of the hotel's last remaining amenities. The human victim was Lord Kimberley, originally Jack Wodehouse, a young man about town upon whom it is probable that his cousin, P.G.Wodehouse, modelled Bertie Wooster. He was Winston Churchill's private secretary at the time of his death as well as being a supreme polo player and chairman of the Bath Club. He died in one of the Duke Street flats and Shane Leslie, a firewatcher at the time, remembered: 'I made my way down Jermyn Street, which was blocked with rubble and glass. Poor Jack Kimberley had just been carried out of his flat unrecognized. . . . I dreaded to find Rosa a victim, but found her seated in a chair in a porch being served with cups of tea.' In fact the bomb had brought down the ceiling in her famous parlour, destroying forever most of the nostalgic paraphernalia. She was not hurt but considerably shaken and so the *Evening News* of 15 May 1941 was wrong in one respect when it reported:

THE CAVENDISH HIT
West End Hotels Bombed
    'The Cavendish in Jermyn Street, Garland's Hotel in Suffolk Street and Store's Ancient Chop-house in Panton Street were badly damaged in recent raids.
Seventy-eight-year-old Mrs Lewis, who has been proprietress of the Cavendish for more than forty years, was injured.'

The important amenity that was destroyed was the Hammam Baths, a place where Cavendish guests could receive services no longer in operation at the hotel. At the Cavendish you could no longer have your shoes cleaned or suits pressed. Neither could you have a manicure or a haircut. And even the bathrooms were now antiquated and hot water was in doubtful and erratic supply. At the Hammam Baths all these things could be had – until the bomb. As a result of this Rosa's customers now had to face the fact that if they drank too much and had to stay the night, then they arose to a bleak morning. To wake with a hangover in one of those chilly Edwardian rooms with no room-service and inadequate plumbing was something of a challenge.

The destruction of the Baths was the result of the second bomb, two days after the first, which also damaged the Cavendish. Whilst the hotel was being repaired Rosa and Edith moved into the Hyde Park Hotel where Rosa, no doubt, gave the staff hell. Mrs Izzard remembers how deeply hurt Rosa and Edith had been that the Ritz refused to give them shelter. The Ritz, however, was possibly one of the hotels which had suffered Rosa's personal visits some years before the war and her outrageous behaviour was all too fresh in their minds.

But with Rosa once back at the Cavendish, the situation soon returned to normal. The Reverend Walter Hannah remembered those black-out parties: 'How Rosa loved them; for she loved seeing people happy, and making them happy; and for her they were doubtless nostalgic of the really great days of the Cavendish in the 1914–18 war. I remember one in particular with Bruce Otley, of the Covent Garden Opera, clowning deliciously with his own very clever composition on the piano, and leading the choruses of Rosa's favourite bawdy song "Three Old Ladies Locked in the Lavatory".'

The same man, who was the curate of St James's, Piccadilly, was responsible for the conversion of Mrs Lewis to God. The bombing, the anticipation of more damage, and her isolation from the modern world were contributory factors. So was her age, and Rosa turned to religion in old age as many thousands of people had done before her. Typically she wanted her priest under her own roof, and she removed him from uncomfortable quarters in Vauxhall Bridge Road to the old Eden apartments in Duke Street. As will be remembered, these had their own separate entrance and showed no obvious connection with the hotel itself – so at least Hannah need not sully his reputation as a man of the Church by living in such an abode of sin as the Cavendish! Also, and probably more to the point, Rosa only charged him a very modest rent, as befitted one who wished to keep her father confessor by her side.

Nevertheless, on Rosa's orders, Hannah was forced to socialize in the Cavendish. As a result of her commands, he paints this picture of Rosa in her old age: 'I would either find Rosa alone and bored in her famous front parlour papered with fading photographs of faded celebrities, drinking a champagne cocktail, with a banana or possibly a sandwich in her other hand, or else crowded with people I'd never seen before, whose names Rosa never got right anyway, when she attempted the introductions.' Hannah also remembers that her catchphrase at the time was, 'People only come to the Cavendish to bounce cheques and pee!'

Rosa began to attend Evensong on Sunday evenings, despite the fact that the inevitable Kippy had to come too – and indeed Hannah remembers the dog's rushing up the aisle and sniffing at his feet whilst he was reading the lesson – which became something of an endurance test for him. She would ensure that her clients came to the service, and Rosa was usually helped in, for she was very frail now, by two of the younger members of the Cavendish set. Hannah remembers that she didn't always stay throughout the service but wandered away and returned – usually with two different supporters:

'Looking down into the Church, I saw Rosa, each hand in a vice-like grip on two Bright Young Things on either side of her, getting into a pew. She stayed a few minutes, and then got up and walked out. A few minutes later, she returned with two more, but by that time the first couple had escaped. So it went on all during the service: she never managed to keep more than four at the most at a time; like the Labourers in the Vineyard, they had all returned to claim their wages, of champagne cocktails. Towards the end of the sermon, she brought in her first two at the eleventh hour, and I (and everyone in church) heard her shout to the Verger "Leave that door open, and let's have some bloody air".'

Hannah was particularly impressed by the manner in which Rosa was able to play a whole series of roles and assume a large number of different identities. For instance, she behaved like a bishop's widow when she met the conservative and innocent Rector of St James's. He was so impressed that he advised Hannah to visit the Cavendish as much as possible so as to be under the safeguarding wing of such a delightful old lady. She also behaved in the same way to Hannah's parents, who were equally impressed.

Rosa still dined out at the Savoy, Quaglino's, the Berkeley and the Ritz, and still behaved as obtrusively as before. She also used the air-raid shelters of the Ritz and the Hyde Park Hotel, and the latter also used to help her out with kitchen supplies from time to time. But as to the real day-to-day progress of the war she was fairly ignorant, as she hadn't been during the First World War. Dimly she saw her 'boys' around her – even if she wasn't always able to identify them.

Dr James Marshall remembered enjoying his visits to the Cavendish but found it difficult to put these singular experiences into words. He noticed that most of the uniforms in the Cavendish came from the army and he surmised that 'perhaps the Navy was too stuffy and the R.A.F. not well-enough bred for R.L., who was certainly a snob'. Rosa regarded Marshall as the Cavendish doctor and he never paid for a drink. Inevitably someone was 'standing treat' although 'he was often lying, asleep or unconscious, on the couch at the far end of the room'. He added that only champagne or whisky was served, nothing was eaten and any outsider was frozen away by a devastating look from Rosa.

Seeing patients in the Cavendish, Marshall was accompanied by Rosa who was, for some reason, dressed in yachting costume. She 'would lead the way at high speed, and then supervised the proceedings, generally disagreeing with any of my proposals. She once called me urgently to see a man who had cut his throat – it turned out that she had misheard him when he said that he would cut *her* throat if she didn't stop hammering at the door.'

Doctor Marshall concludes by pointing out that not all the guests at the Cavendish realized its reputation, nor were a part of its raffish activities. 'One very proper Scottish peer and pillar of the kirk told me he had used the Cavendish all his long life, because it was such a fine, quiet, genteel place – and because R.L. was such a dear old lady.' Marshall once risked taking his wife to the hotel but never again – for Rosa sourly told him that there were plenty of women about the place without introducing wives!

Major S.E.G. Poynders remembered the progress of Rosa's senility: 'Towards the end of the war she wandered about Jermyn Street in carpet slippers and was much attracted to the very good-looking young curate from the church facing her hotel. Her memory failed, and the last time I saw her in her chair she did not recognize me but her welcome was as sincere as it had always been.'

Colonel D.V.M. Wakely, from the Rhine Army, remembered her during the middle of the war years. He was particularly impressed by the freedom of the atmosphere at the Cavendish – as well as the freedom of the drink. He also recalled:

'One evening I was standing in the hall, waiting for a trunk call. Rosa came up to me and said, "What are you doing, young man?" I told her. "Well, go and do the black-out curtains on the landing and in the hall. I'll shout for you if the telephone rings." I complied and reported completion. "You haven't done the window half-way up the stairs," said Rosa. "Go along and do it."

On another occasion, I had just arrived from Alton Towers, Staffs., where I was an instructor at an OCTU, which had been established there in the war. "Where are you now?" asked Rosa. "I'm at Alton Towers," I said. "Oh, you've got Alton Towers, have you?" said Rosa. "I'm glad you've bought it back from the Railways." It was quite impossible to make her understand that I did not own Alton Towers. I was then treated to a discourse on the Shrewsbury family (the original owners of Alton Towers).'

Towards the end of the war Wakely brought his wife to the Cavendish. She had the typical short shrift wives received in the hotel. A double room had been booked – but only a single room reserved. Luckily the matter was resolved by Edith, who pushed out 'the suitcase and pyjamas of a presumably single occupant, who had been given a double room'.

The strain of being an idiosyncratic hostess, a friend, a confidante, a hotel proprietor, a socialite, a snob and a highly courageous woman was beginning to tell. Nevertheless, Rosa's spirit was still as strong as ever. Colonel Hargreaves remembers her standing on the roof with him, shovelling incendiary bombs into buckets of sand as they dropped. The incendiaries were difficult to deal with as they often fell in a cluster, scattering a hundred bombs over a single street. They made a curious plop-

plopping sound and would drift along the roads like autumn leaves. But Rosa was very unimpressed by them and simply referred to the bombs as a 'dratted nuisance'. Hargreaves also remembers how, released from Colditz, he turned up at the Cavendish broke, filthy and pending further military duty, where Rosa lent him £500 in cash, saying 'Don't pay me back till the end of the war'.

One of the most haunting memories Molly Izzard has of the Cavendish of this period is of the time of the Ardennes offensive: 'There was a thick pea soup fog outside and it drifted into the rooms of the Cavendish. There was a sinking sensation in the pit of everyone's stomach, a lot of feverish packing, and it was as if the antheap had been finally overturned. It was an unpleasant, haunting experience – similar to how I imagined the eve of the Battle of Waterloo to be.'

Rosa Lewis was no Lottie Crump and Waugh's cruel satire was never true. Certainly she may well have continually asked her customers to 'have another little drink, dear'. But far more often she was their spiritual and financial comforter – as well as their close friend. But Rosa couldn't keep up the pace – no one could. And at last even her iron resilience cracked. In 1944 Rosa entered a nursing home. She was seventy-seven.

The war was desperately slow in finishing. In July 1944 the diary of one London woman gloomily read: 'Absolutely nothing of note this week; fog, which made me lose my way coming home and fall over the pavements to be rescued by a kindly soldier, ice and frost . . . the usual accompaniment of bangs from rockets . . . sirens one evening early and two doodles . . . droning over the house . . . a hateful boil on my neck . . . People in the office have colds, pains and aches in limbs and crawl about with overcoats on and shawls draped about them . . . With only cardboard and mica windows and no doors or walls to keep out the draughts it is pretty freezing and it seems our legs will never be felt again.'

In the Cavendish Edith carried on during Rosa's convalescence. The drink was in shorter supply, but was still there. The food, thanks to continued country patronage was also still there, if irregular. Elsewhere shortages were severe. Boxing Day fare in another West End hotel took the form of a dried-egg omelette and cold apple tart, whilst a few weeks earlier the Lord Mayor's banquet had taken only half an hour to eat.

Then, after some official shilly-shallying, the end of the war was announced by Winston Churchill at 3 pm on Tuesday, 8 May 1945. One woman who listened to the broadcast in the Westminster W V S shop wrote that after the National Anthem had been played and everybody had gone, she sat on 'alone with Mrs G. We heard the short service which followed. Mrs G's eyes were fixed miles away – on her two dead sons'. Later, the King ended his evening broadcast by saying, 'From the bottom of my heart, I thank my peoples for all they have done, not only for themselves, but for all mankind.'

Rosa, however, was hardly aware of all this for she had finally slipped almost entirely back into the past. This came about by her spending some months recuperating at Longleat with her old friends Daphne Vivian and Harry Weymouth, better known as the Marquess and Marchioness of Bath. She was a welcome but exhausting guest and her reminiscences flowed like the champagne she still drank prodigiously. She was very frail, her memory was poor, but it was at its best in her Edwardian past. Weymouth's mother was Violet Mordaunt and this set off a stream of memories about the Mordaunt divorce scandal and Edward VII's involvement. Also Daphne Vivian's stepmother's family were the Lycett-Greens, who were prominent amongst those involved in the Tranby Croft scandal. So Longleat became a catalyst to Rosa's Edwardian nostalgia and it was from this fountain that she found enough strength to return to the Cavendish.

In post-war years the shabby old hotel continued to function in much the same way as it had done during the war. The crowds were the same (except that they now included the young aristocratic sprigs of the fourth generation), the extraordinary system of paying was the same, the atmosphere of decadent homeliness in Rosa's front parlour was the same. Between the end of the war and Rosa's death in 1952 hundreds of distinguished public figures passed through the Edwardiana of the Cavendish. The ill-fated Commander Crabbe (who was later to go missing, having allegedly been seen swimming as a frogman near the Russian flagship when the Soviet fleet visited Portsmouth) stayed at the Cavendish for some months, living it up on a legacy. He left behind him a good number of IO Us. Tennessee Williams stayed there, as did Epstein and, of course, Nancy Cunard. The writer Michael Voysey, lonely and seeking company after serving as an army officer during the war, arrived in the Cavendish and was befriended by Rosa, whose character he was later to use in a BBC Television serial based on the Cavendish, called 'The Royalty' and starring Margaret Lockwood. He got the impression that she heartily disliked the third (or was it the fourth) generation of effete young aristocrats who hung around her parlour. In her view they had not won their laurels – not been through enough to be acceptable to her. She gave Voysey advice in the usual Lewis style and lectured him on the importance of not being afraid of love.

An American guest of Rosa's, Henry Rye, found the Cavendish to be a very battered place when he stayed there after the war. 'The hotel', he wrote, 'was partly in ruins and Rosa Lewis was definitely not very clear in her mind ... She was a strange sight in those days, wandering about in her dressing-gown like a ghost.' He went on to point out that the inside of the Cavendish 'was a maze of passages and I believe some of the rooms had secret doors. The last room I occupied in the Cavendish had a great pole set in a tub to support the roof right in the middle of the room.'

Mavis de Vere Cole wrote in her diary of Rosa's last declining year at the Cavendish in 1952: 'Only a line while I await a rather uncertain Cavendish dinner. There is a slightly West Highland touch in the roundabout way in which one asks and receives favours here. Very time-consuming, which, I suppose, is the main factor in keeping at bay all the nasty scurrying people who live in other hotels. Rosa is chattering away like anything next door; she seems to have occasional bursts of energy to relieve her somewhat static existence.'

On 7 February 1950 Rosa wrote a letter to *The Times* which may well have broken a long silence from a once famous cook, but which in no way reflected the culinary style of the Cavendish – which was non-existent. Sometimes, and for certain periods, meals were served, but they were of the plainest and simplest English variety. Her letter read:

CATERING FOR AMERICANS

Sir,

To try to do the impossible and imitate other
countries is absurd. Good plain cooking is really the
best, and the best requires no trimmings. My idea of
plain cooking is that, wherever possible, the article
should be cooked when in season and should not be
cut up. Let the potato or the truffle stand up on its
own and be eaten whole. When I visited the United
States, I found American food outstandingly good
but, in my experience, porterhouse steak and roast
beef in the United States are underdone and allowed
to stand on their own without a lot of trimmings. If
we are to entertain Americans in this country we
must concentrate on good plain cooking and nothing
but the best. They must never be allowed to think
that we are trying to offer them the second-rate.

Yours faithfully

Rosa Lewis

The end came suddenly. In the early fifties Edith, with her
sister Maud's help, had installed Rosa's bed in a suite that led
directly into her parlour. There she would be shifted from bed to
chair, and chair to bed. Just after being Confirmed, on 19 November
1952, such an operation was in progress. Rosa was now
eighty-five. Gently Maud and Edith had taken her from her bed
so as to change the sheets. Equally gently they placed her in her
famous chair. When they turned back she was dead. She had gone
out quietly on a tide of memory, content that her beloved and
glorious past should swamp her.

Her funeral was an extraordinarily moving occasion and it was
attended by a glittering array of public figures. The streets were
closed for some distance around and the service, in St James's, was
just as Rosa would have wanted it. Crowded. Her body was then
taken to Putney, where Edith had already bought ground for
both of them in a large public cemetery.

But Rosa's death was not the end of the Cavendish, for the lease
still had some years to run. At first the heart-broken Edith could
not face carrying on the hotel without the all-embracing persona

of Rosa. But at last Maud persuaded her. So the hotel and its predictable clientele continued, but Rosa's parlour was empty, her chair was empty and there was no Kippy curled at her feet, or more likely padding into some place where he was bound to cause disturbance or embarrassment – to the delight of his mistress. For ten more years Edith ran the Cavendish, until the lease came up – and then the hotel and its contents were sold. The Cavendish had been left, in Rosa's will, to Edith and to two of Rosa's cousins, but it had been easy enough to buy them out. The furnishings had been left to Edith exclusively and many of these were sold or given as mementoes to many of the grieving Cavendish clientele.

One rather macabre event occurred to mark the last death throes of the Cavendish. A few days after it was cleared and vacated, a film company took it over to make a movie called *The Party's Over*. This sudden, ironic flurry of activity is best described by Maureen Cleave in her article in the *Evening Standard* of 17 October 1962:

The Party is Over
by Maureen Cleave

'They call this the Kaiser's Suite. It lies concealed behind a mirror in the passage that turns out to be a door. You would never know it was there. There is a drawing-room, a bedroom and a bathroom. Not many people have been inside. They say the suite was for royal guests only – the royal guests of Rosa Lewis, that fascinating Edwardian beauty who ran the Cavendish Hotel like the mistress of a private house for nearly fifty years.

Rosa died in 1952. They say it was through the influence of Edward VII that she was established at the Cavendish. She left it to her friend and companion Edith Jeffrey, but Miss Jeffrey left earlier this year when the lease expired.

Now the pretty Regency building in Jermyn Street with the little garden in the courtyard is about to be pulled down.

Already it looks as if nobody cared. The walls are khaki with dirt.

But today the film people who are making "The Party's Over" moved in and did the house a last service – they tarted up the Kaiser's suite. They painted it blue and gold, put tapestries on the walls, carpets on the floors, flowers in the vases and – as the producer told me with feeling – £4,000 worth of furniture in the room.

The film is about what the director, Guy Hamilton, likes to call "young people who have opted out of Society".

"Now for this shot we wanted a luxurious hotel. Claridge's would have done, but then they would hardly let us pin these lights on the ceiling. Whereas it doesn't matter what we do in this old place. Cost us quite a lot to do it up like this; but I couldn't resist the proportions of this room."

This evening they move all their stuff out, leaving only the bath in the Kaiser's Suite, which is labelled – fittingly enough – *Shanks Fin de Siècle.*'

A few years later, a piece in the *Evening Standard* Londoners' Diary of 24 December 1969 gave a final epitaph on the Cavendish:

CARD-DELUGED

'Habitués of the old Cavendish Hotel, in Jermyn Street – the hotel run by Mrs Rosa Lewis, who died in 1952 – will be pleased to have news of Mrs Lewis's lifelong friend, Miss Edith Jeffrey, who carried on the hotel until 1962, when it was demolished to be replaced by the present Cavendish.

Miss Jeffrey is well and currently being deluged with Christmas cards from friends who knew the Cavendish. She is as present in a Southampton nursing home.

ENSHRINED

She advertised last week her own Christmas greetings to her friends, hence the current deluge of cards at the nursing home.

The Cavendish was, of course, one of London's best-known and best-recorded hotels. Edward VII used to dine there. So did Sir Winston Churchill. Evelyn Waugh enshrined it in his *Vile Bodies.* And other past customers included the Duke of Windsor, Sir William Eden (father of Lord Avon), Lord Lovat, Isadora Duncan, Ellen Terry, Tallulah Bankhead and Fabian of the Yard.'

So the gaunt shell of the Cavendish awaited the demolition squad. Mercifully they were not long in coming and the very last living remnant of the Edwardian era unwillingly died. As the walls crumbled those final ghosts of hectic gaiety had their last pathetic, defiant shout. Somewhere in the wreckage there must have been a last, broken champagne bottle. If not – there certainly should have been.

EIGHT

A Question of Identity

'I was not a favourite child. I was not an affectionate person; and
I was very independent.'

ROSA LEWIS

THE PRESENT POPULAR – ALMOST OBSESSIVE – INTEREST IN the lives of servants at the turn of the century stems from the fact that most of our grandparents *were* these servants. Only a few of us have the heritage of blue blood. One of the most idealized of those servants was Rosa Lewis. But what her disciples don't realize is that she was forced to invent herself. In fact she really had no other choice. Her family background was arid and un-loving. To make her way, as millions have to, without parental and family love, was a tortuous path. Unlike many, she survived, but not entirely intact. Her *petit bourgeois* first employers, the Mus-graves, had allowed her nothing but repression although it is obvious that she spent her years with them growing up very quickly. She was both independent and ambitious but it took her some time to realize that her ambition could be fulfilled as a servant rather than as a schoolmistress. For much of her time at the Musgraves' was spent dreaming about a 'new' life, free of domestic drudgery. But she was still only very young when she realized that this was a dream – and would remain a dream. Nevertheless the ambition burned as strongly as ever and it was then that she decided the only way to real success lay in becoming a super-servant.

Her rise to a commanding position came amazingly quickly and her period with the Comte de Paris turned her from a maid of all work into a young woman of considerable power. Her rapid command of kitchen French, her tenacity, her ability to learn quickly, her talents as a cook and an organizer, made her em-ployers and their friends realize that Rosa was a 'find'.

But with such a commanding situation in London society, a new problem cropped up that she was not expecting – the question of her own identity. Everyone around her was larger than life with personalities to match. But who was she? No more than an efficient servant. Only as interesting as the food on their plates. It was not enough. So Rosa seized on her youth, her spirit, and the 'cockney' background that was patronizingly bestowed on her by the high and often mindless society she was serving. She began to act up to it – to be 'pert', 'spry' and 'cheeky'. The more she did it, the more they loved it, and in this way she achieved a very positive identity for herself, that of the cockney sparrow. Her young good looks helped this considerably and her inherited dislike of men kept those at bay who would make complications. She accepted the arranged marriage and her job as discreet concierge of Edward's apartments as merely a further ladder rung to further success. It is true that she was completely amoral in this sense but there was every reason for this wilful, unloved and therefore unloving young girl to behave in this way. The only true love she ever had was for Edith and Maud, and this, of course, was to occur considerably later in her life. This is not to say that she wasn't kind and her attitude to her own employees was both friendly and compassionate. She had been a lonely person and she loved working in a team – particularly when it was a successful team.

Her attitude to her husband was a strange one. She certainly couldn't tolerate his company and it is very doubtful whether she had any sexual relations with him. But, curiously, she extended her rough kindness to him as well. Excelsior was an object of her pity and perhaps guilt, for there was no doubt that his family was right – the synthetic marriage had wrecked his career. His mishandling of the Cavendish finances, however, received no mercy from Rosa, for she was understandably highly materialistic. One of Rosa's great loves, however, was rebuilding.

Rosa Lewis was an Edwardian to the last. Firstly, she had been brought up with the values of the period. Secondly, she had her greatest successes in the period. For her, post-Edwardian times were a long and colourful decline. But unfortunately the Edwardians were 'not very nice people'. They lacked the moral (if repressive) fibre of the Victorians, many of whom were genuinely concerned with 'good works'. Edwardian high society, and in particular Edward's set, was entirely bent on pleasure. They may well have infected the country with a mood of greater gaiety than dour Victorianism had allowed, but on the other hand they did

not make it a better place. They were insular, complacent, selfish
and unaware of anything else but their own amusements, which
were invariably expensive. So the values they gave to the independent but emotionally immature Rosa were nothing short of
disastrous. At the same time, because of her social position, she
entirely missed out on the new thought that the Edwardian age
brought to the more intelligent strata of society.

As much as Rosa was to regret the passing of Edward's reign,
T. H. White, in his *Farewell Victoria*, regretted its arrival: 'Nevertheless, in the days between 22 January and 1 February in 1901,
something was passing out of England ... Devonshire House,
Staffordshire House, Montagu House, Grosvenor House; something went from them with a rush, downwards, to disappearance,
like water from a bath. The level sank silently; became vocal in
the last moment, dying with a hideous gurgle as King Edward
with his rout came tumbling in.'

With Edward's death came the end of Rosa's social importance. It was a blow from which she never recovered. From that
moment on she began to live in the past and she remained, of
course, in both character and dress a determined Edwardian. She
also retained her invented identity but now it was so much part of
her that not only could she not separate herself from it, but it had
taken over her original personality.

The advent of Eden and Ribblesdale into her life brought out
the best in her and the mixture of tenderness and aggression made
the relationships very binding ones. She achieved a strange kind
of domesticity with the haunted Ribblesdale and their walks in the
park, their shopping trips, theatre outings and the pastoral idyll
with the Tree sisters at Robertsbridge brought Rosa as near to
marriage and to love as she ever would be. As for motherhood,
she came as near to that as she ever would be with her beloved
boys of the First World War. Here she performed the greatest
service she had ever done for human beings – or would ever do
again. As with Eden and Ribblesdale she gave generously all she
had, and this giving had nothing to do with ambition, or success,
or materialism.

The ensuing hard work to repair again the Cavendish fortunes
and the companionship of Edith blotted out the acute pain of the
deaths of so many of her boys, but the feeling of uselessness was

now deeply embedded. That was something that Edith couldn't penetrate, but she did uncover something else where nobody, including Ribblesdale, had ever succeeded. For Edith, and her sister Maud, discovered the real Rosa behind the cockney sparrow image – and in doing so, made Rosa rediscover herself. With Edith and Maud, Rosa was non-abrasive, homely, ordinary and loving. She gave as much as she took, which is well illustrated by her concern for the welfare of the old Mrs Jeffrey. Rosa and Edith were complete opposites which, of course, helped considerably. They understood each other completely. Edith had cracked the code but would never give her away. Rosa knew Edith to be a restrained, retiring woman who needed company. They suited each other, and began to depend more and more on each other as the years of Rosa's long decline rolled by. In the final period Edith was to manage Rosa as Rosa had tended to manage her. Their roles were reversed and Edith became a zealous watchdog, attacking anyone who should lead her beloved Rosa astray.

A number of people mentioned in this book have commented on Rosa Lewis's contempt for her clients and this certainly existed – particularly after Ribblesdale left the hotel. Many of them were obviously contemptible – others more subtly so. Some were not, and it was this group that Rosa tried not to pillory. Her bad behaviour in public places, her bullying and her foul mouth were part of this contempt – and part of her image. The same applies to her robbing-Peter-to-pay-Paul style of charging and also to her idiosyncratic favouritism and antipathies. The poor, wretched journalist Mary Lawton was led a terrible dance over her interview with Rosa, yet writes obsequiously in her foreword:

'. . . Rosa, without any warning, announced that she was ready to begin! I could hardly believe my ears.

After dancing attendance upon her for days and days without apparently any result, she had finally promised of her own accord to really talk the following morning. The miracle had happened. Rosa was going to speak – at last!

I arrived at her appointed hour with high hopes, but alas! to be received not by Rosa, but by the patient William, her butler, who, with a still longer face, informed me in the most courteous English that Mrs Lewis had gone down to Brighton, he thought, or some such place, the night before, and would not be back that day!'

Any contact with the press was regarded warily by Rosa, for she was insecure enough to imagine, somewhat paranoically, that they might in some devious way 'find her out'. Hence her childish reaction to Mary Lawton's naïve transcript and her continuous campaign against journalists. To Rosa, it must have seemed that all her worst fears had come true when she was parodied in *Vile Bodies* as Lottie Crump. Despite her open outrage and anger towards Waugh, there was absolutely no doubt how deeply she was hurt – just as hurt as she was when the Ritz predictably refused to give her house-room after the Cavendish was bombed. It could well be said that she asked for this kind of treatment but it still seems cruel. The trouble is that although being a 'character' may well bring jocular admirers, it is only in a few cases that any kind of friendship is achieved. One such friendship was Daphne Fielding's for Rosa – a relationship in which there was unique give and take.

The Bright Young Things stood no chance of taking over the private section of Rosa's heart that was *in memoriam* to her boys, but they did hold a very strong place in her affections. They laughed at her jokes and laughed even harder at her explosive statements. Some of them probably laughed at Rosa, but either she blinded herself to it or alternatively she ignored it. She thoroughly enjoyed queening it at Cowes, playing the grand old lady, being rude to the pompous yachtsmen and having more genuine week ends at Jevington. The company of the Bright Young Things made her feel alive again and it was just possible that, when she was very drunk, she could detect a resemblance in some of the young men to those earlier young men who had lain terrified in their trenches, a packet of Rosa's goodies still in their knapsacks and memories of her comfort still in their hearts.

As we have seen, the Second World War was largely a confusion to Rosa and although she was very generous to the officers in the Cavendish, offering a convivial bolt-hole for them and their families, she was very much out of touch with what was going on. She now tended to live more and more in the past and to rely on Edith to run the hotel. Although she obviously drank a good deal of champagne she was certainly not an alcoholic, although continued toping made her recognition of the present and its personalities even fuzzier. Most of her clients accepted her version of their identity or personality, and soon became used to the names from the past by which she called them.

Rosa seemed to be an old woman for an incredibly long time and during the period between the end of the Second World War and her peaceful death in 1952 she marked time, whilst the old hotel did the same around her. As she nodded over the Cavendish fire, she shared her days with Edward and the Kaiser, with Eden and Ribblesdale, with her boys and with her memories of what it had been like to be young and important and needed. Now she was only an old London character, who could get away with anything – and often did.

Rosa Lewis was discreet to the end of her life. Although she was nostalgic, she rarely gossiped about the past to anybody. She simply lived it in her own mind. Rosa has a specific importance in social history, not just of the Edwardian period, but of the years up to the end of the Second World War. At the height of her success she was unique in being not only the most famous cook and kitchen manager in Europe and probably America too, but also a woman who could be trusted by the highest echelons of society – admittedly for nefarious reasons. Not everyone could claim to be the Prince of Wales's favourite cook *and* his concierge. At the same time she was unique because she rose to power as a woman just when the first flutterings of a tenuous emancipation were perceptible in Edwardian households. And although you couldn't say that Rosa Lewis was emancipated (she spent too many years serving men to be that), because of her independence, fortitude and abilities she rose to a position in the catering world of the time that no other woman could have occupied.

Rosa's creation, the Cavendish, was the final example of her importance. Here she not only retained the Edwardian aura, but provided an atmosphere in which the elite could disport themselves more or less (subject to Rosa's approval) as they wished. But it was not just this that made the Cavendish significant. It was the fact that it attracted some of the most famous names of the century and built up a roll of honour, and dishonour, second to none. It provided respite to the war-scarred, comfort to the lonely, discretion to the devious, and frivolity to the frivolous. Like its owner it was unique. But unlike its owner it had an identity that was entirely genuine. It was only for Rosa that identity was in question.

Bibliography

Aberconway, Christabel, *A Wiser Woman?* (1966).

Acton, Harold, *Nancy Mitford* (1975).

Asquith, Margot, *Autobiography Vols 1 and 2* (1920).

Baily, Leslie, *BBC Scrapbooks Vol 1: 1896–1914* (1966); *Vol 2: 1918–1939* (1968).

Battiscombe, Georgina, *Queen Alexandra* (1969).

Beaton, Cecil, *Diaries 1948–55: The Strenuous Years* (1973).

Bedford, Sybille, *Aldous Huxley: A Biography. Vol. 1* (1973).

Bentley, Nicolas, *Edwardian Album* (1974).

Brander, Laurence, *E. M. Forster: A Critical Study* (1968).

Branson, Noreen and Heinemann, Margot, *Britain in the Nineteen Thirties* (1971).

Briggs, Asa, *They Saw it Happen* (1960).

Bromley, Gordon, *London Goes To War – 1939* (1974).

Brook-Shepherd, Gordon, *Uncle of Europe: Social and Diplomatic Life of Edward VII* (1975).

Brough, Leslie, *The Prince and the Lily: Edward VII and Lily Langtry* (1975).

Carstairs, Caroll, *A Generation Missing* (1930).

Cartland, Barbara, *We Danced All Night* (1971).

Cecil, Robert, *Life in Edwardian England* (1969).

Churchill, Peregrine and Mitchell, Julian, *Jennie: Lady Randolph Churchill* (1974).

Cooper, Lady Diana, *The Light of Common Day* (1959).

Cowles, Virginia, *Edward VII and his Circle* (1956).

Crewe, Quintin, *The Frontiers of Privilege* (1961).

Dangerfield, George, *The Strange Death of Liberal England* (1966).

Davidoff, Leonore, *The Best Circles* (1973).

Delgado, Alan, *Have You Forgotten Yet?* (1973).

Dickson, Lovat, *H. G. Wells: His Turbulent Life and Times* (1969).

Eden, Timothy, *The Tribulations of a Baronet* (1933).

Fielding, Daphne, *Mercury Presides* (1954); *The Duchess of Jermyn Street*

(1964); *Emerald and Nancy, Lady Cunard and her Daughter* (1968); *The Nearest Way Home* (1970).

Flanner, Janet, *London Was Yesterday* (1975).

Fleming, Kate, *The Churchills* (1975).

Glyn, Elinor, *Three Weeks* (1908).

Harrison, Michael, *Rosa* (1962).

Heckstall-Smith, Commander, *Sacred Cowes* (1965).

Holroyd, Michael, *Lytton Strachey: A Biography* (1971); *Lytton Strachey and the Bloomsbury Group: His work, Their Influence* (1971).

Hughes, M. Vivian, *A London Family Chronicle* (1950).

Hynes, Samuel, *The Edwardian Turn of Mind* (1968).

Izzard, Molly, *A Heroine in her Time* (1969).

Judd, Denis, *The Life and Times of George V* (1973).

Langtry, Emily Charlotte, *The Days I Knew* (1924).

Lawton, Mary, *The Queen of Cooks – And Some Kings* (1925).

Leslie, Anita, *Jennie* (1969); *Edwardians in Love* (1972).

Leslie, Seymour, *The Jerome Connexion* (1964).

Leslie, Shane, *The Anglo-Catholic* (1929).

Longmate, Norman, *How We Lived Then* (1971).

MacQueen Pope, W., *Back Numbers: A Disturbance of the Dust of Yesteryear* (1954).

Magnus, Sir Philip, *King Edward the Seventh* (1964).

Malcolm, Thompson George, *Lord Castlerosse* (1973).

Mannin, Ethel, *Young in the Twenties* (1971).

Margetson, Stella, *The Long Party* (1974).

Masters, John, *Fourteen Eighteen* (1965).

Middlemas, Keith, *Edward VII* (1975).

Montgomery, John, *1900: The End of an Era* (1968).

Mosley, Nicholas, *Julian Grenfell* (1976).

Mowat, Charles Lock, *Britain Between the Wars: 1918–1940* (1955).

Owen, Roderic with Tristan de Vere Cole, *Beautiful and Beloved* (1974).

Pearsall, Ronald, *Edwardian Life and Leisure* (1973).

Petrie, Sir Charles, *Scenes of Edwardian Life* (1965).

Pike, Royston E., *Human Documents of the Age of the Forsytes* (1969).

Pound, Reginald, and Harmsworth Geoffrey, *Northcliffe* (1959).

Powell, Violet, *A Substantial Ghost* (1967).

Priestley, J. B., *The Edwardians* (1970).

Pryce-Jones, David [Ed], *Evelyn Waugh and His World* (1973).

Raglan, Lady, *Memories of Three Reigns* (1928).

Read, Donald, *Edwardian England* (1972).

Ribblesdale, Lord, *Impressions and Memories* (1927).

Roby, Kinley, *The King, the Press and the People* (1975).

Ryan, A. P., *Lord Northcliffe* (1953).

Sackville-West, V., *The Edwardians* (1930).

Sassoon, Siegfried, *Memoirs of an Infantry Officer* (1930).

Smiles, Samuel, *Self Help* (1859).

Summerson, John, *Georgian London* (revised edition) (1970).

Sykes, Christopher, *The Life of Lady Astor* (1972); *Evelyn Waugh: A Biography* (1975).

Symons, Julian, *The Thirties: A Dream Revolved* (1960); *Between The Wars: Britain in Photographs* (1972).

Taylor, A. J. P., *From Sarajevo to Potsdam* (1966).

Thompson, David, *England in the Nineteenth Century* (1950).

Tweedsmuir, Lady, *The Lilac and the Rose* (1952).

Waugh, Evelyn, *Vile Bodies* (1930); *Ronald Knox* (1959).

White, T. H., *Farewell Victoria* (1933).

Willis, Frederick, *A Book of London Yesterdays* (1960).

Wilson, Angus, *The Naughty Nineties* (1976).

Wilson, Barbara, *Dear Youth* (1937).

Windsor, Duke of, *A King's Story* (1951).

Winter, Gordon, *The Golden Years 1903–1913* (1975).

Index